One of Paul's greate[...] church was that their pure and undivided devotion to Christ would somehow become corrupted by the preaching of a different Jesus. Paul's specific words to them were, "You happily put up with whatever anyone tells you, even if they preach a different Jesus than the one we preach" (2 Cor. 11:4, NLT). In many ways, I have that same concern for the church of today.

To preach another Jesus is to preach an incorrect version of Him, a different Jesus than the One depicted in the Bible. You may wonder how on earth this could happen. No Christian in their right mind would blatantly accept a false Jesus, right? If someone came along teaching that Jesus is not the Christ, He never died on the cross, He didn't overcome the grave, this would be obvious heresy. However, the deception is subtle.

So how have we preached a different Jesus? By what we've failed to communicate. In present times we create a "Jesus" who will give us whatever our passions desire— much like Aaron did for Israel when he fashioned the golden calf and called it Jehovah. The children of Israel still acknowledged the name of God and the fact that He saved them from Egypt, but they changed Him into a different Jehovah.

In the same way, anytime Jesus is depicted as just Savior (and not Lord), we are presenting a Jesus that offers salvation on our terms. This means we believe we can have the benefits of His salvation without relinquishing our lives to Him. The Jesus of the Bible clearly commands that we must deny ourselves, take up our cross, and follow Him. When we make Jesus Lord, He becomes our Savior as well.

Jesus as Savior emphasizes forgiveness of sins and redemption; Jesus as Lord translates to a complete reorientation of one's life. When we preach Jesus only as Savior, we're preaching a different Jesus. That's why so many unbelievers come to Jesus just for what He can do for them. Jesus becomes just another means to an end, rather than the end of all means.

That's why I'm so happy my friend Jonathan Stockstill has written *The Real Jesus*. More than ever, we need a fresh revelation of Jesus—one that will set our hearts ablaze and reignite a holy fear within us. Only then will we truly know Him! The truths contained throughout this book will empower you to give Jesus the place in your heart He deserves.

—JOHN BEVERE
BEST-SELLING AUTHOR AND MINISTER
COFOUNDER, MESSENGER INTERNATIONAL AND
MESSENGERX

Jonathan Stockstill's *The Real Jesus* is a must-read book about the One who has been the center of conversations, agreements, disagreements, misunderstandings, much love, and occasionally deep hatred in some people's minds and hearts. You simply must immerse yourself in its content to discover, understand, relate to, and fall in love with Him. *The Real Jesus* will lead you on an exciting journey of following Jesus as His disciple.

—ELIAS DANTAS
FOUNDER AND INTERNATIONAL FACILITATOR,
GLOBAL KINGDOM PARTNERSHIPS NETWORK

The Real Jesus is a profound yet practical and contemporary book. Why? Because this is exactly what Jesus is! Thus by presenting such important facets of Jesus in the light of the Word, this book also brings us principles that should guide the life of every Christian.

You will be led to a journey of knowledge, reflections, and very practical applications for your life. You will be called to decisions about deliveries to be made, understandings and values, your heart and your actions and influence on others. You will find that you will no longer be able to know Jesus without being transformed by Him.

This book will provoke you to reflect on your past and your future, relationships, compassion, service, forgiveness, and so much more. But all the topics point in the same direction, which is to ask, Are you willing to, by faith, place Jesus at the center of your life?

—CARLITO PAES
LEAD PASTOR, THE CITY CHURCH,
SÃO JOSÉ DOS CAMPOS, SÃO PAULO, BRAZIL;
FOUNDER, THE CITY CHURCH NETWORK AND THE
INSPIRE DE CHURCHES NETWORK

One of the greatest phrases that Jesus ever said was "Follow me!" Pastor Jonathan Stockstill is a leader that our nation and generation can follow. God never intended for us to follow only principles but to follow a life. Jonathan's life can be followed because he follows Christ.

—JUDE FOUQUIER
LEAD PASTOR, CITY CHURCH CALIFORNIA

Discipleship is not *said*; it's *seen*. Jonathan Stockstill is the living proof of three generations of discipleship, seen and embodied in a grandfather and father who have discipled many of the key leaders in the body of Christ today.

—JACOB ARANZA
PASTOR, OUR SAVIOR'S CHURCH

THE REAL JESUS

JONATHAN STOCKSTILL

CHARISMA
HOUSE

Visit the author's websites at https://bethany.com/ and https://jonathanstockstill.com/.

Library of Congress Cataloging-in-Publication Data:
An application to register this book for cataloging has been submitted to the Library of Congress.
International Standard Book Number: 978-1-62999-991-3
E-book ISBN: 978-1-62999-992-0

21 22 23 24 25 — 987654321
Printed in the United States of America

CONTENTS

ACKNOWLEDGMENTS

I REMAIN FOREVER INDEBTED to my beautiful wife, Angie. Her ceaseless encouragement pushes me to believe I can do whatever I set my hands to do. I also want to thank my kids, who inspire me not only to talk about but to know the real Jesus; and Bethany Church, which is living these truths out in community. Finally, special thanks go to Marcus Stumvoll, Max Davis, and Amy Dunn for helping make this project a reality and pushing me over the finish line.

FOREWORD

I F EVER THERE was a time for the church to stand strong and make an unprecedented impact worldwide, it's today. God is calling *you* to take a deeper look, not at your battlefield or even your purpose or your next assignment, but at who Jesus is and what He is asking you to do. If you are truly going to make a difference in this world for the Lord, then knowing Jesus Christ and obeying His teachings are the first steps in your process.

It's safe to say that 2020 was a year like no other. With the onset of a worldwide pandemic in early spring, what we thought was a temporary setback became months of evaluating and reevaluating priorities and a complete overhaul of everything from the way industry does business to the way we interact socially across all spectrums. Likely everyone has experienced the devastating effects of COVID-19 in one way or another, either personally or by way of a family member or close friend. Millions of Americans found themselves out of work, and the financial markets shook worldwide. In 2020 we had to learn to adjust and evolve.

The same was true for churches. That's why when many churches were closing their doors for good, others grew in ways they never could have imagined and took giant leaps forward, accomplishing things that would normally have taken years. As you launch deep into all that is next, there is no time like the present to reevaluate *your* priorities. God is calling you to take bold steps of action and has chosen *these* days to be *your* days. He is inviting you to see Him like you have never seen Him before so that you can do things you never would have been able to do. In other words, you were born for this moment, and God is calling you to play a part in all He is about to do in the earth.

Every great journey, every unforgettable adventure starts with the first step. It's time to take inventory of the instructions God has for you for the next leg of your journey. Lesson one is to know Jesus. To know Jesus— really know Him—means you can distinguish Jesus' voice from everyone else's. To fully know Jesus instills in you an uncommon faith and an unusual peace in every trial and in every attack. To truly know Jesus is to know every battle has already been won by the One who died to make that possible.

There are too many well-meaning believers who hear from God and sense a call on their lives, only to respond, "I'll take it from here, Lord." It's not long before they find themselves on roads they don't recognize filled with obstacles they have no idea how to deal with. Even our greatest soldiers spend months in training before they are ever deployed for the missions they were intended to carry out. *The Real Jesus* is that basic training you need to help you adjust and evolve so you do matter in every situation and every life you encounter.

God is looking for people who will get off the sidelines of observation and analysis and get in the game and be counted as part of something bigger than you could imagine. He's calling you to something God-sized even, because "bigger than you could imagine" is exactly where we find ourselves today, in a world trying to navigate uncharted waters. Spend some time in each chapter. See each page as a road map taking you one step closer to the heart and mind of Christ. See every moment spent reading the book as God filling you with His Holy Spirit and filling your mind with the faith and confidence you will need for any mountain or Goliath you might find along the way.

The real Jesus is waiting for you, and your greatest testimonies are yet to be experienced. It is time to know more about Him!

—JENTEZEN FRANKLIN
SENIOR PASTOR, FREE CHAPEL

FOREWORD

ONE OF THE privileges of getting older has been watching my children and the children of family and friends grow up and become adults. I'm always fascinated to see the through line of the person God created them to be emerge in infancy and grow into maturity. And I'm especially intrigued by the ways parents and caregivers try to pass on their faith in God to the next generation. That's because no matter how devoted to Christ someone may be and how diligently they raise their children in the faith, their children's spiritual development is not entirely in their hands.

As a pastor and a father myself, I know there's a limit to how much I can ultimately influence the faith of my kids. They have to experience God firsthand and discover His love beyond what human love and conceptual understanding can reveal. When they struggle through life's challenges and wrestle with what it means to follow Jesus, it can be especially heartbreaking to watch them make painful choices. On the other hand, when they push through tough times and discover God's faithfulness for themselves, when they grow and mature into a faith that's uniquely theirs, it's incredibly inspiring.

Even more inspiring is when they become pastors and leaders whom God uses to bless countless others as they share His love and use their gifts in His service.

Such is the case with Jonathan Stockstill, whom I've known for most of his life. Jonathan is the son of my pastor, Larry Stockstill, and I've loved seeing Jonathan grow from the little boy running through the pews after church to a passionate pastor, dynamic leader, and exuberant praise-and-worship artist.

While some people might assume Jonathan's passion for ministry was inherited, I know he continues to build on his dad's legacy and make it uniquely his own. This starts with the foundation of his faith, his relationship with Jesus Christ. Jonathan discovered that sometimes when you're raised in a devout Christian home, the pressure to conform to the expectations of others, especially those in the church, can be tremendous. It can be difficult to discern when you're trying to please your parents and others by accepting the customs of their faith versus when you're motivated by knowing and loving God at a deeper, more intimate level.

Jonathan quickly learned that you can't settle for an inherited set of beliefs if you want to make a difference in this world. You have to answer the fundamental questions at the heart of this book: Who is Jesus to me? What do I really believe about who He is? And what difference does it make in my life—right now and for eternity?

Jonathan knows these are the honest, gut-level questions every believer must answer for himself or herself in order to have an authentic, loving relationship with God and to live with passionate purpose in His service. That is why Jonathan has written this book—to help you and me and everyone come to terms with the real

Jesus, to cut through what others say and what we see and hear in our daily lives and on social media.

As Jonathan points out, even during Christ's time on earth, many people offered different opinions about this carpenter's son from Nazareth who claimed to be the Messiah, God's own Son. At one point Jesus even asked His disciples, "Who do people say the Son of Man is?" In reply, they listed some of the rumors floating around: "Some say John the Baptist; others say Elijah; and still others, Jeremiah or one of the prophets" (Matt. 16:13–14, NIV).

Now, what's striking here, as Jonathan explores, is the number of assumptions people made about who Jesus was. Rather than listen to what He said and experience His teaching and healing for themselves, many people just identified Jesus by association, by hearsay, by speculation. "Yeah, I think He's that crazy guy John, who runs around in the wilderness eating locusts and honey," some apparently said. "Or what about one of those prophets from hundreds of years ago, like Elijah or Jeremiah, the ones who did all those big dramatic supernatural spectacles?" others must have chimed in.

With these assumptions on the lips of the public, Jesus then asked His disciples, "But what about you?... Who do you say I am?" To that Simon Peter replied, "You are the Messiah, the Son of the living God" (Matt. 16:15–16, NIV). Jesus then blessed Peter for his faith because "this was not revealed to you by flesh and blood, but by my Father in heaven" (Matt. 16:17, NIV). In other words, Peter didn't rely on earthly evidence— and he certainly witnessed plenty of miracles while accompanying his Master's ministry—but on supernatural revelation.

Through the power of the Holy Spirit, we can also encounter God's presence and the truth of who Jesus is for ourselves. We don't have to rely on hearsay, popular culture, or the church we attended as children. We can get to know the living God in a way that's personal, direct, and intimate. Jonathan knows the difference and provides a map to help you experience the power of relationship over religion, of a higher purpose over personal glory, of joyful contentment over elusive happiness.

Whether you inherited a solid biblical foundation for your faith or you're still searching for the truth about God, *The Real Jesus* will open the door to a more intimate encounter with the Savior. With humor and honesty about his own struggles to overcome childhood "Biblianity," fresh insight on what God's Word actually reveals about Christ, and practical encouragement for deepening your relationship with the Lord, Jonathan challenges you to experience Jesus in ways that require you to risk more of your heart.

If you're tired of settling for what others say about Jesus Christ, then it's time to decide for yourself. Ask Him to show you who He is, and you won't be disappointed. And don't be surprised if He uses this book to show you new glimpses of His character, power, and unconditional love for you. If you truly want to encounter the real Jesus, then keep reading!

—CHRIS HODGES
SENIOR PASTOR, CHURCH OF THE HIGHLANDS

FOREWORD

I HAVE ALWAYS BEEN fascinated with discipleship.

Having been a lead pastor for twenty-eight years and preaching for fifty-two years, I've watched many people come and go. Many lacked the roots, the relationships, and the character conversion to make the Christian journey to the end.

I love this book. It is a signal that the new generation "gets it." I watched my son Jonathan as he really entered discipleship as a teenager. He led our worship team at the age of seventeen. In his twenties, he found a wonderful life partner in Angie. He traveled the world doing worship and started his family of five children.

At thirty he entered a whole new phase of leadership as he and Angie became the lead pastors of Bethany Church. Now, almost ten years later, he is ready to share the new-generation values he has curated in his first forty years of life.

What we read in this book is real stuff.

The new generation is all about reality: reality shows, social media posts, and "Show me the difference it makes." Here is Discipleship 2021. It is our new generation recording their love for Jesus in a fresh, new way. It is knowing God the Father, Son, and Holy Spirit intimately. It is channeling Christ's love, forgiveness, and servant attitude practically. It is taking up the torch of Christ to let it be seen in the darkest corners of the world brightly.

This book tells me that the gospel is in good hands in the new generation. They are leading powerful churches with high creativity and compassion. They are writing intimate music that comes out of their deep passion for prayer. They are on fire to bring the gospel to the final unreached people groups and hasten the coming of the Lord.

Use this book for yourself. Use it to disciple your new-generation (and old-generation!) church members in a way that is real and challenging. With a world as crazy and desperate as we are living in, whatever you do, *use it*! Train disciples who become leaders who multiply disciples.

My heart is filled with joy at what the next forty years will look like in Christianity. I want a front-row seat.

—LARRY STOCKSTILL
FOUNDER AND DIRECTOR, PASTORS UNIVERSITY

INTRODUCTION

A JOURNEY OF DISCOVERY

Seeking Authentic Faith

T O SAY I was raised in a Christian home would be an understatement. My dad, grandfathers on both sides, and many close family friends were pastors. I faithfully attended Sunday school and was in church every time the doors opened: Sunday mornings, Sunday nights, and midweek for worship rehearsals. I was taught every Bible story—Noah, Samson, Elijah, you name it—including the obscure ones. I even invented a term for the fun of it: *Biblianity*. My religion was the Bible. Growing up, I was surrounded by church people and church programs. This came with significant advantages but also significant challenges. I often saw other people's deep, spiritual, and genuine relationships with Christ as nothing more than the cultural norm. It was our tradition. It was no big deal.

It didn't occur to me until much later in life that all my training in Biblianity was trying to point me to the central figure of Christianity. From Genesis to Revelation, Jesus is the focus of the whole thing! I can't say I had an aha moment when this became clear. It was a progressive understanding. I could ride the coattails of my dad's and grandfathers' faith for only so long. My big struggle was to own my biblical training for myself. Christianity, I realized, was all about Jesus—who He is, what He did, what He taught, and how that matters to me!

One day I came across John 14:23, which said if I loved Jesus, I would obey His teaching. I pondered the power of that statement. Here, I had been trained in the Ten Commandments; I knew all about the nation of Israel, the Jewish law, the prophets, and even end-time prophecy. But the main focus of my life should have been *knowing* Jesus Christ and *obeying* His teaching. Then a question floated up in my mind: Did I even know what Jesus had taught? And a bigger question, Did I obey what He taught?

The apostle Paul said it best after listing his plethora of achievements and knowledge: "Everything else is worthless when compared with the infinite value of *knowing* Christ Jesus my Lord."[1] Being an authentic Christian is not complicated at all. It simply means to be a Christ follower. We follow Him by pursuing a relationship with Him through His Spirit, obeying His teaching, and becoming more and more like Him.

As the lead pastor of Bethany Church in Louisiana, one of my quests has been to teach the congregation who the *real* Jesus is. With this in mind, I worked with a team of pastors and teachers to simplify what Jesus claimed about Himself, how He related to the Godhead, and what He taught and expects of us. The result was a ten-week series that became the inspiration for this book.

If you're hungry for the truth, this book is for you. It's for seekers wanting to know just who Jesus Christ is. It's for those unsure of what it means to follow Jesus and in need of a guide to become serious disciples. And it's for those who have settled into religious routine and want to deepen their understanding of Jesus and experience more of His presence.

Wherever you are in life, now is the time to throw open the doors and discover all Jesus has called you to be. I encourage you to use this as a tool in your own discipleship and in the discipleship of others. This book is all about the *real* Jesus!

PART I

JESUS—THE EPICENTER OF EVERYTHING

1

A MOUNTAIN OF A QUESTION

Relating to Love

[Jesus] asked His disciples, saying, "Who do
men say that I, the Son of Man, am?" So they
said, "Some say John the Baptist, some
Elijah, and others Jeremiah or one of the
prophets." He said to them, "But who
do you say that I am?"
—Matthew 16:13–15

I KNOW THIS SOUNDS radical, but God visited me a
few years ago in a night vision. I believe it was God
because it was life altering. In the same way Jacob
in the Book of Genesis saw a staircase to heaven in a
dream and realized God had been with him, I knew God
had visited me.

In the vision, I was seated in a large auditorium similar to a theater or church. It was filled to capacity and
lively with conversation, though there was no one yet
on the stage in front of us. Someone shouted, "He's
here!" My head turned to see what the commotion was
all about. I couldn't make out a physical form, but a
vaporous shadow moved up the aisle from the back of
the room toward the front. A field of energy and streaks
of lightning surrounded the giant shape, and everyone

remotely close to it shrunk in their chairs under the magnitude of its power.

As the form got closer to the stage, I could make out a person, a man. There was no question as to the identity. It was Jesus. He was at least ten feet tall. The authority and power I felt from Him was indescribable. I had the sense I was in the presence of the ruler of the world. Yet He was smiling and laughing as He walked. Victory best describes what I felt. I was in the presence of the glorious Creator in human form, and His joyful and confident laugh filled the room like a lion's roar.

Throngs of people ran to Him, many falling on their faces and worshipping, others just trying to touch Him. I stayed in my seat, partially because I was under the weight of His presence and also because I would never have been able to get close to Him amid the commotion.

Then Jesus turned and looked me in the eyes as if I were the only person in the room. "Jonathan!" He called, motioning for me to come.

Shocked that He knew my name, I froze.

"Yes, you, Jonathan," He reaffirmed, His voice filled with kindness.

I slowly stood and moved toward Him, but it felt like I was wading through wet cement. I could hardly walk, and the closer I got, the harder it became. Tears streamed down my face. Barely able to contain my emotions, I pressed forward, and the crowd parted. By the time I reached Him, Jesus had to catch me because I was collapsing. He held me close, and I realized I was only as tall as His abdomen. Even to a 6'2" man, Jesus seemed huge!

After gathering myself, I blurted out something

that seemed irrelevant in hindsight. "I've been writing songs for You."

He smiled. "I've heard every one, and I love them!"

I felt silly for allowing that to be my first statement to Him, but it was what it was. I could tell He loved me even more than a man loves his own child. I was over-whelmed with a sense of acceptance like I had never felt in my life. It was true agape love.

In that moment, I instinctively knew it didn't matter how hard I had worked for Him. That's not why He loved me. Nothing I had done or ever would do could earn His love. Nothing. I desperately needed that understanding. It set me free. My whole life prior, I had worked for His acceptance. I had tried to earn His plea-sure. But in this encounter, I realized He loved me just because I am His. He *is* love. He loves each of us before we ever love Him.

"Can I pray for you?" Jesus asked, while holding me up.

I was confused. He was God. Whom was He going to pray to? Then I was reminded that He lives to make intercession for us.[1] Yes, Jesus prays to the Father for us.

I nodded.

As Jesus prayed, a surge of power rushed through my body, jolting me upright and onto my feet. It felt like someone put a high-pressured air hose in me and inflated me to maximum capacity. I felt invincible. The Book of Revelation says John fell down as a dead man before Jesus and then Jesus strengthened him. That's very similar to what happened to me. The experience gave me a new perspective of the balance between Jesus' authority and His love. When you are His and

5

you are with Him, you realize that power is *for* you and not against you. It's working on your behalf.

Finishing His prayer, Jesus gently moved me aside, smiled, and said, "There are others who need My attention." He stepped away and started praying for others.

After the vision ended, I went into the bathroom and just sobbed. For days I was under the weight of this visitation. It's forever imprinted on my mind and will always be a reference point in my life. From that point on, Jesus truly became my focus. Not religious performance, not programs and activity, but simply Him. Now when I lead worship, my goal is to see Jesus with the eyes of my heart and to help others see Him as well. I want them to experience Him like I did, because He really is the solution to everything we face. Now when I preach a sermon or lead a song in worship, He is my focus.

A true encounter with Jesus has the ability to transform you forever. If your heart is open, it's impossible to see Him as He really is and remain unchanged. My prayer is that in the chapters to follow, the picture I paint of Jesus and His teachings will revolutionize your life. Are you ready for something more? Will you let Him show Himself to you? If so, you will no longer be able to see Christianity as just another religion or cozy social structure by which to live your life. Jesus will change you from the inside out. You will never be the same.

That's what this book is all about—discovering who Jesus is, what He taught, how He lived, and how He relates to God the Father and to people. Whether you're an atheist, an agnostic, a seeker, or a Christian, you have a mountain of a question to face.

Who is Jesus?

———❖———

Moving is one of my least favorite things in the world. It's a painstaking process to pull each thing out of its closet or cabinet, organize the mess into categories, and box it all up. What's really difficult is knowing where to put the items that don't fit any category. Should I put the DVDs with the antiques, the electronics, or the trash? Inevitably, there is a box labeled Miscellaneous. It ends up being a catchall for batteries, charging cables, old photos, scissors, and other odd items. By the end of the process, everything is in boxes, and each box is marked to define its contents.

Let's face it. As humans, we often want to define things. We tend to put them in boxes, categorize them, and give them names. We also do this with people. As early as elementary school, kids know each other by clothing styles, interests, wealth, abilities, and social standing. And once people get categorized, it can be difficult for them to erase that from others' minds.

I remember someone in high school who wanted to switch from being a cowboy to a gangster. He went from wearing tight Wranglers and boots to wearing baggy pants and chains. It was like he was playing dress-up. Although he changed his outer appearance, we still knew him as a cowboy and could never make the mental switch. To this day, if his name is mentioned, I instinctively think cowboy, not gangster. It's a human tendency. We like to categorize things and people to determine their relationship to us.

So, what is the nature of your relationship with Jesus? To what category do you assign Him? Where does He fit in your life?

Seriously, this is *the most important question* you will ever answer.

And no one else can answer it for you.

When you hear the name of Jesus, what comes to mind? Or to put it another way, who do you say Jesus is? In your heart of hearts, do you question whether the stories in the Bible are all myths? If Jesus did exist, was He just a man? Was He a prophet? A great teacher?

Or was He something more?

Your answer is critical. Your eternal soul depends on it.

If you're an atheist or agnostic, this question is a key that can unlock doors in your mind. If you're a seeker, it can open your heart even wider. And if you're a Christian, it can move you from a neutral, passive religion into a vibrant, active life with God.

Most people want to avoid the question. Sure, they might believe Jesus was an actual person, but if pressed to answer who He *really* was, defenses go up. Through a chuckle or a shrug, they say, "I don't know." They put Him in the miscellaneous box. I think at the core of this response is the possibility that Jesus really is the Son of God. If He is, it changes everything. He said that He came to save the world from sin.[2] For many, He evokes a sense of shame, of anger, or of feeling overwhelmed. If you pull up a YouTube video or a popular blog post about Jesus, you're likely to find an ocean of comments about the delusion of Him and His followers. Sometimes I peruse those comment threads just to see the status of people's hearts. It blows me away how many people hate Christians and hate Jesus, the Christ.

Some label Him as a fraud.

Others say He was simply a good person.

To answer the question of who Jesus really is, you must be hungry for the truth about Him and about yourself and be willing to follow that truth. If He is who He claimed to be, you can't afford to deal with it later.

Who is Jesus to you?

IN A COMPLETELY DIFFERENT CATEGORY

No single person has impacted the history of the world as much as Jesus Christ. It's not even close. If you google "Jesus" on any given day, you'll get over nine hundred *million* results. Around 75 percent of the world's population has heard the name of Jesus.[3] His face has been depicted in many different forms. Some paintings represent Him as a White man with long hair. Others portray Him as a Black or Middle Eastern man. There are even paintings of a Chinese Jesus. Some pictures show Him with short, curly hair and a rugged, muscular build. Others depict Him as a gentle soul. Regardless of the form, people tend to recognize Him. They might even say out loud, "That's Jesus."

The fact He existed as a man and walked the earth is not even up for debate. Historical scholarship has ended that argument. Professor Tom Wright, senior research fellow at Wycliffe Hall, Oxford, wrote, "From time to time people try to suggest that Jesus of Nazareth never existed, but virtually all historians of whatever background now agree that he did."[4] I could go on and on with similar quotes from top scholars, so I'm not going to debate whether or not He was real.

Just think about it. Jesus was a lowly Jewish carpenter from an obscure little town. He lived only thirty-three short years. Walking was His principal mode of transportation, so the area He traveled was extremely limited. There were no cell phones, newspapers, TV, or social media to promote His message. News traveled primarily by word of mouth. Letters took weeks, sometimes months, to arrive from distant regions. On top of that, Jesus was just an average, plain-looking Jewish man. The Scriptures tell us, "There was nothing beautiful or majestic about his appearance, nothing to attract us to him."[5]

All the above is true, and yet time itself is defined by His existence. We have BC and AD. Even atheists use calendars that say AD 2020. But two thousand twenty years since when? Since Jesus Christ. AD stands for *anno Domini*, Latin for "in the year of the Lord,"[6] a reference to Jesus' birth. BC simply means "before Christ." There's the world before Jesus, and there's the world after Jesus. He is the epicenter of history. He is the epicenter of everything. If you ask me, that is the hand of God at work. Time is not divided by the birth of any other person. Jesus is the only one.

Jesus.

He stands at the center.

Muhammad, Buddha, Gandhi, Abraham Lincoln,

Billy Graham, Shakespeare—these are people who wielded great influence over the centuries. Yet Jesus is in a completely different category. To believers, His name is beautiful and precious. To unbelievers, His name is a stumbling block. You never hear people say "Oh, Buddha!" when they are angry, "Oh, Muhammad!" when they stub their toes, or "Oh, Gandhi!" when something goes wrong. It's always "God [blank]!" or "Jesus Christ!" Have you ever pondered why? Could it be that there's a weight and power in His name like no other? That God and Jesus are inseparably linked? Also, we have a very real adversary who wants Jesus' name—the only name by which a person can be saved—to be trampled.

Jesus' own disciples had to decide what they believed about Him. They watched Him change water into wine, walk on water, heal the sick, and cleanse the lepers. They even watched Him raise the dead. I mean, they saw some crazy stuff. And then came that moment when Jesus was about to go to the cross to be crucified. It was the point of His ministry and the whole reason He came. He looked at His disciples and wanted to know, "Guys, who are people saying I am? How are they categorizing Me?"

The disciples answered, "Some say John the Baptist, some Elijah, and others Jeremiah or one of the prophets."[7] Although Elijah was an Old Testament figure, certain Jews believed in a form of reincarnation by which great prophets could once again walk among the living. Some found it easier to believe Jesus was Elijah reincarnated than to believe He was the actual Son of God.

Jesus then asked His disciples, "But who do *you* say that I am?"[8]

For all of us, that is the most important question.

Perhaps you think you aren't ready to categorize Him just yet. But if you can't do it now, what makes you think you'll be able to later? Later may never come, and it's much too important to delay. The way you answer the question will change everything.

If you're not sure of the answer, why not ask Jesus to show Himself to you in a new way? He doesn't speak just to pastors and worship leaders. He wants to reveal the depths of His forgiveness, power, and love to each of us. He wants us to know who He really is and what He actually taught instead of us relying on opinions, rumors, or scriptures taken out of context.

This book is your catalyst to change. This very date on the calendar is based upon Jesus' factual existence. You cannot remain neutral. His influence is all around; it's impossible to ignore. So why put Him off any longer? If you don't already know Him, He wants you to experience for yourself His life-changing love. And if you do know Him, He is ready for you to walk in deeper obedience, doing the good works God has prepared for you.[9]

Are you ready to meet the *real* Jesus and become all He has created you to be?

MAKE IT REAL

- Did you grow up in church? If so, did this create in you a deeper desire to know Jesus and His teaching? How has it affected your daily life? Discuss with a friend the ways Jesus and His teaching impact your home, your neighborhood, and your country.

- If you did not grow up with biblical teaching, what makes you want to know more about Jesus? Have you come across conflicting views of Him? Consider reading and discovering His true nature in the Gospels—Matthew, Mark, Luke, and John.

- Ponder Jesus' impact on human history. How would the world be different if He had never walked the earth? If you still question His historical existence, do an online search for proofs, and consider how Jewish and Roman history point to Jesus Christ.

2

A MOUNTAIN OF EVIDENCE

Relating to the Truth

Simon Peter answered and said, "You are
the Christ, the Son of the living God." Jesus
answered and said to him, "Blessed are
you, Simon Bar-Jonah, for flesh and
blood has not revealed this to you,
but My Father who is in heaven."
—MATTHEW 16:16–17

GROWING UP, I was surrounded by siblings. There were six of us, and it was wild! We had so much fun, activity, and competition around our house—and yes, sometimes friction. "Who said?" was a question we asked a lot. One of our brothers or our sister could run out and yell at those of us who were playing, "Everyone, get inside right now!" Our immediate response would be that two-word question, "Who said?" We wanted to know by whose authority the command was given. If our sibling just said it on his or her own, we had no obligation to obey, but if our parents sent the word, we knew we'd better hurry in or face the consequences.

Before we go any further in this book and consider the things Jesus taught, we need to know on whose authority He acted. If He was a liar or a crazy man, there's no need to follow His teachings or shift our priorities. But if He was God in the flesh, we should seriously consider every word He spoke. This was also an issue for the leaders of Jesus' day. They wanted to know who had sent Him and on whose authority He did the things He did. Many times, He made claims about Himself that were about as far out there as you could get. He said that He acted and spoke on His own authority and on His Father's, but that wasn't good enough for His doubters. They couldn't see His Dad, and like my siblings and me, they demanded to know "Who said?"

Years ago I had a friend who earned quite a reputation for making far-fetched claims about himself. I'm pretty sure we've all known someone like that. He told story after story about how he had evaded certain death, jumped off roofs, made and lost thousands of dollars, stumbled upon secret hideouts of notorious criminals. You name it; we heard it. He became so infamous for his tall tales that we called out his first name whenever somebody lied or exaggerated.

Throughout time, people have made ridiculous statements about themselves. I remember as a twelve-year-old boy watching the news about the ranch in Waco, Texas, where David Koresh died in a showdown with federal authorities. Koresh claimed he was the son of God, but it was obvious to me even at age twelve that he couldn't be telling the truth.

In Jesus' day, many thought of Him as a liar, an exaggerator, and a false prophet. When you consider some of the statements He made about Himself, you can understand why. Think about it. What if the guy working next to you suddenly declared himself to be God and really believed it? You'd have him committed.

Here are some of the outrageous claims Jesus made about Himself.

"I am the light of the world."[1] Wow. In John chapter 8, Jesus essentially says the world is floundering in darkness and confusion. If you have Him, you have the light and you are no longer lost. But if you don't follow Him, you are in the dark. What a bold claim! That's some serious arrogance—unless you really are who you say you are.

"I am the way, the truth, and the life. No one comes to the Father except through Me."[2] In a world of universalism and empathy for all religions, this is a hard one. This statement excludes anybody who doesn't come to God through Jesus. According to Jesus, it isn't enough to believe He is *a* way to God. He claims to be *the* way. The only way.

"I am the resurrection and the life."[3] Almost every religion believes in some sort of afterlife. Whether it's through reincarnation, becoming one with the universe, or reaching nirvana, everybody wants to peer beyond the veil of death and see what's on the other side. Jesus simplifies it all, saying if we will believe in Him, He will personally ensure our resurrection after death. Dying is one of people's top fears, and Jesus claims to be the solution to that fear.

"I have been given all authority."[4] Over whom? To do what? Jesus states here that He has no restrictions. He has supreme authority over every spiritual entity, all of creation, and even time itself. He is where the buck really stops. In this verse, He declares His sovereignty.

I have always existed.[5] From before Jesus was born, He was! He speaks to His Jewish listeners about Abraham, and when they ask how He could have seen Abraham, He replies in John 8:58, "Truly, truly, I say to you, before Abraham was born, I am" (NASB). Not only does Jesus make clear that He was around before Abraham, but He also calls Himself by the same name God used while speaking to Moses from the burning bush: "I AM."[6] Jesus talks about what life was like before the universe began. He speaks of seeing Satan cast down to earth. He mentions knowing men who lived thousands of years before Him. Abraham, Isaac, and Jacob were His personal friends. Can you imagine knowing someone who claimed these things?

I am the final judge.[7] Ultimately, every angel, demon, and human will be judged by Jesus.[8] He gets the say on who is allowed into eternity with God and who will forever be separated. If this claim of His is correct, it drastically simplifies our lives. All we really need to do is please Him. I heard a story once about the late-night talk-show host Johnny Carson. When new comedians appeared on his show, they were encouraged to focus not on the crowd or the cameras but on Johnny. That's because if he liked them, he would invite them to the couch for a conversation. This brief TV exposure could set entire careers in motion.[9] All they had to do was please *one* person—Johnny Carson. On a much larger scale, Jesus is the one we need to please. He is the final judge, the one making the judgment calls.

I am God.[10] Jesus never claimed to be just a prophet.

He told His listeners that He had been sent by His Father and that He and the Father are one. If His other statements didn't already make Him look crazy or arrogant, equating Himself with God was a way for Him to get Himself killed. "We're stoning you," the Pharisees told Him, "not for any good work, but for blasphemy! You, a mere man, claim to be God."[11] Although Jesus avoided death that day, this is the same accusation that eventually got Him crucified.

The political and religious leaders of Jesus' day couldn't accept Him because His identity threatened their positions and authority. Others tended to believe Him because they watched Him heal the worst diseases, raise the dead, cast out demons, walk on water, and feed thousands of people. When He spoke one on one to individuals, He often did so prophetically, seeming to reach inside their souls and address their most heartfelt needs.

In John 4, when Jesus talked to the woman at the well, she must have thought He'd been reading her mail. After blowing her mind by knowing her marital and relational history, He said, "If you only knew the gift God has for you and who you are speaking to, you would ask me, and I would give you living water.... Anyone who drinks this water will soon become thirsty again. But those who drink the water I give will never be thirsty again. It becomes a fresh, bubbling spring within them, giving them eternal life."[12]

Wow, what a claim!

Jesus didn't give her counseling or advice. Instead, He offered Himself as the solution to every problem she was facing. He was the answer she had been looking for, and she believed Him.

The demons also believed—and they trembled. Throughout the Gospels, the demons screamed out Jesus' identity whenever He got close to them. He burst through their darkness like a brilliant light, which I would compare to a nuclear bomb. They literally couldn't stand to be close to Him. At His command, they came shrieking out of the victims they possessed, declaring that He was indeed the Son of God.

If Jesus' miracles, teaching, and testimony didn't speak clearly enough, He also had His Father backing Him up. After Jesus' baptism in the Jordan River, the Father claimed Jesus as His Son in a thunderous voice from heaven. On the Mount of Transfiguration and after the resurrection of Lazarus from the dead, the Father repeated His affirmation. Those who were around Jesus on these occasions either detected strange, thunderous phenomena that sounded like words or heard with their own ears the majestic God of heaven!

Over five hundred eyewitnesses saw Jesus after His resurrection and before His ascension into the clouds. If His closest disciples did not see Him, why did each one of them die a martyr's death instead of simply admitting He was dead? If He was not truly risen, would His followers have spread a gospel that still encompasses the globe two thousand years later?

Jesus was the real deal. He fulfilled more than three hundred Old Testament prophecies. Professor and statistician Peter W. Stoner, in an analysis reviewed by the American Scientific Affiliation, stated that the probability of just eight of these prophecies being fulfilled in one person is 1 in 10 to the seventeenth power. That's 1 in 100,000,000,000,000,000.[13] Jesus fulfilled three hundred! Think of it this way: out of the estimated 108 billion people who have lived on the earth since the beginning of time,[14] Jesus is the lone individual who divided human history and fulfilled every single Messianic prophecy. It's hard for me to wrap my mind around such staggering odds. Theodore Parker, a transcendentalist and Unitarian minister, is attributed with saying, "It would have taken a Jesus to forge a Jesus."[15] Dr. S. Lewis Johnson quoted Parker, then added, "If it is true that what we have in the Bible is a giant forgery, then let us worship the individual who was so brilliant as to think up a picture of a person like Jesus of Nazareth and the story of the Word of God."[16]

All these things add up to a mountain of evidence that Jesus wasn't just making baseless claims. He had witnesses. There was proof.

How do you perceive His radical claims? For a natural man to make those statements and demands, it's crazy, arrogant, narcissistic, evil, and demented. But for God to make such statements, it is right and proper. In *Mere Christianity*, C. S. Lewis wrote:

> I am trying here to prevent anyone saying the really foolish thing that people often say about Him: "I'm ready to accept Jesus as a great moral teacher, but I don't accept His claim to be God." That is the one thing we must not say. A man who was merely a man and said the sort of things Jesus said would not be a great moral teacher. He would either be a lunatic—on a level with the

man who says he is a poached egg—or else he would be the Devil of Hell....You can shut Him up for a fool, you can spit at Him and kill Him as a demon; or you can fall at His feet and call Him Lord and God. But let us not come with any patronising nonsense about His being a great human teacher. He has not left that open to us. He did not intend to.[17]

In his wonderful book *More Than a Carpenter*, Christian apologist Josh McDowell wrote:

I cannot personally conclude that Jesus was a liar or a lunatic. The only other alternative is that he was—and is—the Christ, the Son of God, as he claimed. But in spite of the logic and evidence, many people cannot seem to bring themselves to this conclusion....The issue with these three alternatives is not which is possible, for obviously all three are possible. Rather, the question is, "Which is most probable?" You cannot put him on the shelf merely as a great moral teacher. That is not a valid option. He is either a liar, a lunatic, or Lord and God. You must make a choice. Your decision about Jesus must be more than an idle intellectual exercise. As the apostle John wrote, "These are written so that you may believe that Jesus is the Messiah, the Son of God, and"—more important—"that by believing in him you will have life" (John 20:31). The evidence is clearly in favor of Jesus as Lord.[18]

If Jesus was a crazy person, the foundation of Christianity would have fallen apart a long time ago.

To date, one of my favorite passages in the Bible is when Paul writes a letter to the church of Colossae and describes Jesus as the exact image of God. As Jesus walked this earth, He was God with a face. "He is the image of the invisible God," says Colossians 1:15–19, "the firstborn over all creation. For by Him all things were created that are in heaven and that are on earth, visible and invisible, whether thrones or dominions or principalities or powers. All things were created through Him and for Him. And He is before all things, and in Him all things consist....For it pleased the Father that in Him all the fullness should dwell."

Did you catch that last sentence? The fullness of God—everything about Him that we need to know—is found in Jesus. If you want to know what God would do, look at Jesus. I love how Bill Johnson puts it: "Jesus Christ is perfect theology."[19]

A WHOLE NEW WAY OF LIVING

Imagine living in the first century, walking the same dust-filled roads, eating from the same *kikkar lechem* (loaf of bread) as Jesus, and actually hearing Him make these wild claims about Himself. Would you have taken Him at His word? Many who saw Him in the flesh still refused to believe. The religious leaders who were looking for the Messiah rejected Jesus and turned Him over to the Romans for crucifixion. To them, He was a blasphemer, a complete fraud.

Today, we have two thousand years of history, apologetics, and the fulfillment of hundreds of Old Testament prophecies to confirm Jesus' identity. We have no excuses. If He's not a liar or lunatic, then He is Lord and deserves our worship, total submission, and obedience. If He is the God who created us and the reason we're all here, then our only appropriate response is to fall to our knees, listen to Him, and take His words seriously. His teaching is not just good advice. It is truth—*the* truth—and should be obeyed like a sovereign command!

Embracing Jesus Christ's teachings can revolutionize and transform your life. The same God who wrote the laws of gravity and thermodynamics wrote the principles spoken by Christ. They are as true and fundamental as creation itself. Unfortunately, too many have only heard rumors about what He taught. They have speculations about Him based on teachings taken out of context. Jesus is the designer of everything that exists. He is the great architect and the master teacher. We can glean truth from others, but when it comes to the way we live, Jesus is the one to follow—not Oprah, Dr. Oz, Dr. Phil, or anyone else.

To be a Christian, a Christ follower, is to adopt His way of life and His instructions. If we do not, are we even living as true Christians? Christianity is not just knowing *about* Jesus. It's receiving His life, submitting to what He taught, and saying, "I'm going to look like that."

Now that we have discovered who Jesus really is, we will spend the rest of this book examining what He really taught. Do you want to know God more intimately? Then you must understand what Jesus says about relating to the Trinity. Do you want to live with a heart of compassion and forgiveness? Is that as hard for you as it is for me? Then it's important to know what Jesus tells us about relating to people. And if you want to live a meaningful and fulfilling life, you'll need Jesus' guidelines relating to purpose.

Ponder the questions below. Take a few minutes to let what we've discussed in this chapter take root in your heart.

Then get ready.

There is no turning back once you decide to be a Christ follower. Truly following Him isn't a comfy, once-a-week event. It's a whole new way of living. The *real* Jesus will challenge you in ways you never imagined, change you from the inside out, and free you to be the real you!

MAKE IT REAL

- Do you believe the claims Jesus made about Himself? Which of the seven listed in this chapter is hardest for you to grasp?

- What is your biggest concern this week? Is it something at home, at work, or in your family? Which of Jesus' claims best addresses your concern? If you have never put your faith in Jesus Christ or seen Him as God's gift to humanity and the Savior of your soul, consider doing so now. You don't need fancy words or a memorized prayer. Speak to Him from your heart. Confess your faults and doubts, then ask Him to renew your heart and mind. This is what it means to be born again.

PART II

JESUS—LEARNING FROM HIM

3

THE INVITATION OF A LIFETIME

Relating to Jesus the Son

> One day as Jesus was walking along the
> shore of the Sea of Galilee, he saw Simon
> and his brother Andrew throwing a net
> into the water, for they fished for a living.
> Jesus called out to them, "Come, follow
> me, and I will show you how to fish for
> people!" And they left their nets at
> once and followed him.
> —MARK 1:16–18, NLT

WHEN I WAS four, my parents allowed me to choose a musical instrument to learn to play. Guitar, trumpet, violin—the choice was mine.

"I'd like to play the piano," I said.

So at the age of four, I began to study piano. For the first year, I didn't learn a whole lot, mostly because I didn't like to practice. Actually, I hated to practice. I told my mom, "You've got to pull me out of this. I want to play sports. I don't want to play piano. Please pull me out."

"Before we do that," she said, "I want to take you somewhere."

My mom took me to a recital at Louisiana State University, where I watched as five- and six-year-olds competed on stage. The winner of that competition studied under a teacher named Eugenia O'Reilly. Next, the seven- and eight-year-olds competed, and that winner's instructor was also Ms. O'Reilly. Then the nine- and ten-year-olds competed, and again, the winner studied under Ms. O'Reilly. When the eleven- and twelve-year-olds competed, the same thing happened. All of the number one students studied with Ms. O'Reilly. I concluded that this woman must be the best piano teacher around.

Ms. O'Reilly had unkempt white hair that looked like it had never been brushed. I mean, it was just big and out there. She seemed eccentric, and as I discovered, that description was spot on. She was bigger than life, and all her students seemed to love her.

I told my mom, "If I'm going to take piano from anybody, I want to take it from Ms. O'Reilly because I want to win."

My mom said OK, and we approached Ms. O'Reilly about it. A few days later, we went to her studio for an initial interview. "Sit down at the piano and play something," she told me.

So I did.

"I'll take him!" she exclaimed to my mom.

I was like, "Yes!"

I went into my first lesson thinking, "Ms. O'Reilly is my best friend. She likes me. I like her. This is going to be a fantastic relationship."

"Jonathan, sit at the piano," she instructed firmly.

I sat and realized the atmosphere was not quite as

friendly as during my interview. She had one of those retractable wands in hand, and I wondered, "What's she going to do with that?"

"Go ahead," she said. "Play something."

I played for about five seconds before she whacked my hands with that wand! "What in the world?" she said. "Your hands are flat. Lift your hands!"

I lifted my hands and started to play again.

Whack!

"Oh, no," I thought. "What have I gotten myself into?" Here, I figured she was going to be the friendliest woman around, and that was just not the case. She did not win competitions by being friendly. Those she accepted as students were entering her world, and she trained them to be really fantastic pianists. But she wasn't trying to be their best friend.

Well, when I was six years old, I entered that same recital competition at LSU. Guess who won? Me. I won again at seven, then again at eight—thanks in large part to Ms. O'Reilly and her stick. She was tough, but she was the best of the best. She set a very high bar. I don't remember my first piano teacher's name or what she taught me, but I remember Ms. O'Reilly.

When you're being trained by the best of the best, it's a big deal and it costs you something. Jesus was the best of the best. A lot of rabbis in Jesus' day taught a lot of things, but none taught like Jesus. Although He was warm and inviting, there was a huge cost involved in being His disciple. To enter His world meant leaving everything else behind. Unlike Ms. O'Reilly, He offered a close relationship in return, but even those closest to Him bowed in adoration when they understood who

He was. For example, Jesus and John were tight. John was the one who rested his head on Jesus' chest. Yet even John fell at Jesus' feet like a dead man when he saw Him in all His glory.[1]

Despite the cost of following Jesus, the benefit is that you actually study under God Himself. You are mentored by the Creator.

What a privilege!

Christianity is not merely a list of rules or a Sunday morning routine. It is a process of studying under Jesus Christ. It is a lifetime of learning personally from Him. It is a matter of coming to Him and saying, "Teach me life. Teach me how to live."

BREAKING THE MOLD

In first-century Jewish culture, the premier religious leaders were called rabbis. As hard as it may be to imagine, the rabbis were the coolest people. They led the way. If you became a disciple of one of the rabbis, it meant a lot for you and your future. And then there were the leaders of the rabbis, the really great teachers. It was huge to be chosen to study with an esteemed teacher of Jewish law such as Gamaliel, whom Saul of Tarsus (Paul) learned under.[2] It was like being the number one pick in the NFL draft.

The selection process began during childhood. Every Jewish boy aged five through twelve studied the Torah, the first five books of the Old Testament: Genesis, Exodus, Leviticus, Numbers, and Deuteronomy. A boy didn't just read the Torah. He memorized it—all five books. By the time he was twelve, he could recite for several hours from Genesis 1:1 all the way through Deuteronomy. Some excelled more than others. The ones chosen to move on got to memorize the whole Old Testament![3] I think I have John 3:16 down. The finest of this group moved on to the next step. Only a select few were chosen to study under one of the revered rabbis. A boy who made it this far believed his future was bright. It was like getting a full scholarship to Harvard or Yale. It was the invitation of a lifetime.

Jesus was recognized as a rabbi, even addressed as "Teacher" by the Pharisees[4] and as "Rabbi" by Nicodemus, a ruler of the Jews.[5] Jesus was smart. He was the cream of the crop. Remember when He was in the temple as a twelve-year-old boy amazing the rabbis? He never stopped surprising and baffling them. He knew the process rabbis used to select their students, yet when it came to His own disciples, He didn't choose only the most learned or the ones considered most likely to succeed. Often He did just the opposite.

Early in the Gospels we find Jesus walking along the seashore, calling ordinary guys. Simon Peter made the cut, though he may not have made it out of middle school. A fisherman by trade, he was casting his nets when Jesus approached him. "Follow Me," Jesus called out. Peter looked up and saw the man people had been calling a rabbi. Imagine Peter's shock when he realized a rabbi was inviting him to be His disciple and study under Him. Peter, of course, dropped his nets.[6]

Jesus also invited Levi, who was a tax collector, a traditionally greedy role. Levi left his table immediately, and Jesus changed his name to Matthew.[7] Matthew later wrote the first of the four Gospels. This is true discipleship, saying, "Jesus, You are my teacher. You are my instructor. You can change me, even change my name, if You want to."

Jesus broke the mold by choosing the ones nobody else would pick. He is still choosing regular, everyday people—even broken ones—to be His disciples and doing extraordinary things through them. This means you and I qualify.

Now, that's great news!

Just as I had the tremendous privilege of training under Ms. O'Reilly and the early disciples had the otherworldly opportunity of learning under Jesus, every Christian today is extended the offer of studying under the master tutelage of the Son of God. Rabbi Jesus is walking by the seashore of your life and calling out to you, "Come, follow Me." You may have failed in the past. You may feel inadequate. Maybe you consider yourself a nobody who doesn't measure up. Jesus is still calling out to you, "Whosoever will, let him come."[8] The original misfit disciples chosen by Jesus eventually turned the world upside down!

Jesus now extends to you the invitation of a lifetime. Will you become a true disciple? He delights in taking ordinary people, nobodies, and misfits and preparing them for extraordinary things. But you must be willing to drop the nets in your hands and take up His teaching.

So what exact steps are involved?

LEAVING

The first step in becoming Jesus' disciple is leaving. It is the hardest part, but you can't ignore it. The next three steps are actually a lot of fun, but this first one is more like Ms. O'Reilly whacking my hand with her wand—a bit painful.

None of those who followed Jesus were able to continue life as they knew it. Peter had to drop his nets, his source of income and sustenance. Levi had to leave his table. Think about that for a minute. Levi was sitting there collecting taxes. There was a lot of money under his table, and he kept a hefty percentage. Then Jesus called him, and he just left the table and money and everything behind and followed Him.

When you follow Jesus, you leave all that's familiar to you. That is the cost of discipleship. You cannot have Jesus and cling to everything else too. When He says, "Follow Me," it's your choice. You can keep fishing. You can keep collecting taxes. You can keep living the way you have lived. Or you can follow Him. But you can't do both.

Know this: there is a stark difference between being an onlooker of Christianity, an appreciator of Christianity, and an actual disciple of Jesus. Many people consider themselves disciples, but being a disciple is totally different from being a fan or simply appreciating something. A lot of people are big fans of boxing or UFC martial arts. I'm always amazed when I watch a match on television. While two guys slug it out like modern-day gladiators, people in the audience act as though they're the ones in the ring or the cage.

They yell stuff like, "Get him! Tear his heart out!" But they're not in the fight. They are safe, just looking on. Christianity is being in the ring. It's not being outside, looking in, and just appreciating or being a fan of the faith. It's not just sitting behind the table and watching. It's putting it all on the line.

Jesus had a lot of fans. He raised the dead, turned water into wine, and fed the multitudes with a couple of fish and a few loaves of bread. People thought that kind of stuff was cool, and they crowded around Him. Yet as His fan base got really big, Jesus often turned and said something hard to swallow, cutting the group to about one-tenth. Only those serious about following Him stuck around. Jesus was constantly throwing down the gauntlet.

I bring this up because it actually happened in the Bible. You cannot read the Gospels and avoid it. In Luke 9:59 Jesus called to someone to follow Him. The person agreed but replied, "Lord, first let me return home and bury my father" (NLT). It's a reasonable request, don't you think? I mean, I love my dad. I surely want to bury him when his time comes. But look at how Jesus answered. "Let the spiritually dead bury their own dead! Your duty is to go and preach about the Kingdom of God."[9] Do you see how tough Jesus made it to be one of His disciples? Another person said, "Yes, Lord, I will follow you, but first let me say good-bye to my family." Jesus replied, "Anyone who puts a hand to the plow and then looks back is not fit for the Kingdom of God."[10]

Look, a lot of people believe in Jesus. They are Christians by title but have not made the massive step of saying, "I abandon everything. I leave everything behind to follow Jesus." Jesus doesn't play around. To be His disciple comes at a cost.

When we leave to follow Jesus, we leave our old identity—it is dead—and take on a new identity. Peter's life no longer centered on being a fisherman; he was a disciple. Levi was no longer a tax collector; he was a disciple. Mary Magdalene was no longer demon possessed; she was a disciple. Someone reading this, perhaps even you, will have to say, "I'm no longer a Wall Street executive; I'm a disciple." Or, "I'm no longer focused on being a star athlete; I'm a disciple." To follow Jesus, you must be willing to leave those things in which you place your identity.

Are you also willing to leave your comfort behind to follow the call of God? A teacher of the law told Jesus, "'Teacher, I will follow you wherever you go.' Jesus replied, 'Foxes have dens and birds have nests, but the Son of Man has no place even to lay his head.'"[11] Comfort may look to you like a secure job. Sometimes Jesus, for His purposes, calls you out of security into a life of instability. You pray that doesn't happen, but it may. One thing is for sure, though. God will call you out of your comfort zone.

Jesus calls us to leave our possessions as well. The disciples left houses, relatives, and occupations to follow Jesus. What if Jesus called you to sell your house? What if He asked you to give away your car? What if He prompted you to give everything away? The rich young ruler wanted to be His disciple, but Jesus said, "Sell what you have and give to the poor...and come, follow Me."[12] The guy walked away, sad and torn.

He wanted to be a student of Rabbi Jesus, but he also wanted to hang on to his stuff. And you can't do both.

Now, I'm not suggesting you close this book and go sell your house and start sleeping on the streets as a way of saying, "I'm a disciple of Jesus." But if He does ask you to sell everything, can you do it? Jesus constantly asked people to leave things behind.

One of the biggest things Jesus calls people to do is love Him more than anyone else, including fathers, mothers, spouses, kids, girlfriends, boyfriends—everyone. Jesus wants to be the center of our love and affection.[13] We really do have to forsake all else to follow Him.

I read a story recently about a Muslim girl who converted to Christianity. It took her almost six months to develop the courage to tell her family she had accepted Jesus, knowing her conversion from Islam was punishable by death. In many parts of the world, a person's relatives will execute them for bringing shame upon the family. It's called an honor killing. Scared for her life, this young woman finally told her parents what she had done. Her dad grew visibly shaken and began to weep. He grabbed her by the arm and threw her out of the house. "Never come back!" he screamed as he slammed the door. She stood on the threshold of her home with no money to her name and nothing but the clothes she wore. Yet she counted it better to forsake everything and live for Jesus than to deny Him for a comfortable life with her family. Today, she still serves Jesus, and God is using her in a powerful way.

Here's the deal: God is calling you out of relationships, lifestyles, and sins that hold you back. He wants you to stop trying to do both the God thing and the world's things at the same time. His call is for you to love Him first, to love His presence more than the people and things of this world. Being a disciple of Jesus starts with leaving.

LEARNING

Learning is the next step in being a disciple. Once you are willing to leave your nets and your table behind, you will get to the good stuff—learning from wisdom personified. By walking among us, Jesus showed us what God looked like. Jesus was God with a face. As God, Jesus is omniscient and omnipresent. There is nothing He doesn't know. He is the embodiment of all perfect wisdom. When you come to study under Jesus, the omniscient One, you are going to learn some things.

You are going to learn stuff about life that'll change your world. I'm saddened by the masses of people who don't walk in the wisdom of Jesus Christ. Oftentimes, their entire lives—marriages, families, careers—suffer because they don't have God's wisdom. But each of us has the opportunity to study under wisdom Himself. Who would not want that?

Jesus says, "Come to me, all of you who are weary and carry heavy burdens, and I will give you rest. Take my yoke upon you. Let me teach you."[14] When most people think of a yoke, they picture an ox or mule carrying it, but there's more to what Jesus is saying. In those days whatever interpretation a rabbi applied to Scripture was called his yoke.[15] When Jesus says to take His yoke upon us, He is urging us to let Him be our rabbi. "Let me teach you, because I am humble and gentle at heart."[16] His instruction will lead not to stress and exhaustion but to relief for your soul.

The world has lots of philosophies. You can get in an argument on just about every street corner over how life is to be lived.

"I think life is a box of chocolates," one says.

"I think it's more like a roller coaster," says another.

"Well, you're both wrong. Life is like a football game."

A ton of different philosophies are out there, but Jesus has a philosophy called "the mind of Christ."[17] When we learn from Him, He gives us a whole new paradigm for thinking—a new philosophy and world-view. Our minds must be renewed to begin to think like Him.

Jesus has an eternal perspective. His mind is not focused on this life but on the next. Likewise, we are here not to gather treasure on this earth but to store up treasure in the kingdom of heaven. Jesus didn't talk a lot about ancient Rome or Israel, but He talked a whole lot about the kingdom of heaven. Here in the United States, many people talk about America, America, America and about what has happened, what is happening, and what should happen in the future. I thank God for this nation and the blessings we have here. But Jesus is not American. He refocuses our attention from this earthly kingdom to His eternal kingdom, which is just as real.

Jesus told us not to worry about this life because if God can clothe the lilies of the field, He can certainly clothe us.[18] You don't have to stress out about money or the world's philosophies. If you hang with Jesus, you will start thinking on a higher level. This is discipleship—learning from Him.

After changing our thinking, Jesus begins to change our character. As we discover from Him what true character is, our lifestyles are impacted. And as our minds are renewed by His teachings, we become transformed into His image. This is what discipleship looks like for those who follow Jesus. He is basically saying, "Come in. Watch Me help people. Watch Me love people." If you read the Gospels, you'll see that is what Jesus did. He walked around healing people, setting people free, raising folks from the dead, casting out devils, and teaching lessons as He went. The whole time, the disciples walked beside Rabbi Jesus, watching Him and taking notes: "Did you see how He did that? Did you hear how He answered them?" They were following the Master, omnipotent God clothed in human flesh, and learning how to serve.

This brings us to the third step.

LOVING

One of the major attributes distinguishing Jesus from other rabbis is that His connection with His followers is not transactional. It's relational. We don't give Jesus money so He will then give us an education. Jesus wants a love relationship. He wants to be your friend. Jesus says, "I no longer call you slaves, because a master doesn't confide in his slaves. Now you are my friends, since I have told you everything the Father told me."[19]

Once we take the first step of discipleship, abandoning everything and leaving our old lives behind, we reach the second step of learning and acquiring all this amazing wisdom. Jesus tells us things the Father has shown to Him. And as we experience more of Jesus, we begin the third step, falling in love with Him and beginning to love others as He does.

In essence, Jesus rubs off on us, and we rub off on others. That's how it works. The apostle John referred to himself as the one Jesus loved, and at the Last Supper, we see John sitting as close as he can to Jesus. It is no coincidence that John's epistles are known for their incredible revelations of the love of God. This love is unquestionably the predominant theme. The closer you are to Christ, the more you will understand that He desires a relationship, not a transaction. As you spend time with Him, you will be transformed by His profound love for you, and through that relationship you will learn how to love others as He does.

Growing in love is a critical element in becoming Jesus' disciple. He said, "Your love for one another will prove to the world that you are my disciples."[20] If we are not growing in that love, we are not His disciples. But it starts with loving God first. Jesus tells us to love God with all our hearts, souls, minds, and strength. We need His supernatural power to accomplish that. As we learn to love God with all that we have and all that we are, we begin to love others as we love ourselves.[21]

In the Bible, Jesus is seen not only as wisdom personified but also as love personified. The world does not know how to love God's way. As humans with fallen natures, we are naturally selfish and self-centered. We focus on our own needs first, but Jesus continually gave. Think about it. Jesus sweat drops of blood in the Garden of Gethsemane, knowing what He was about to endure—agonizing pain and torture beyond comprehension. He was the epitome of love as He gave His life on the cross. And He did it all for us. Jesus said, "Greater love has no one than this, than to lay down one's life for his friends."[22] This is how Jesus loved, and this is how He calls us to love.

When you sit under Rabbi Jesus, love is what you get. His school is your life, and He is handing out degrees in love. Come and get yours!

LEADING

Leading is the fourth and final step of discipleship under Jesus. He doesn't just change us and move on. He empowers us to do exactly what He did.

If you are a disciple of Jesus and you're watching Him, your mind, your character, your heart, and your actions will all be impacted. As He teaches you to love others, something else happens. You begin leading in the body of Christ, helping others learn. Jesus passed along the things He taught, giving His disciples authority to cast out evil spirits and to heal every kind of disease and illness.[23]

Jesus told them, "Most assuredly, I say to you, he who believes in Me, the works that I do he will do also; and greater works than these he will do, because I go to My Father."[24] The same works and greater works? Now, that's discipleship. It's all about following the *real* Jesus and doing what He did. Peter, James, John, and many others who had followed Him for over three years began to teach and heal people in His name. As a disciple of Jesus, you too will move in His authority and grow in leadership.

The pinnacle of discipleship is doing what your teacher does. "A disciple is not above his teacher," Jesus said, "but everyone who is perfectly trained will be like his teacher."[25] A student is not greater than the teacher, but the student who is fully trained will become like the teacher. Ask yourself, Am I looking like Jesus? Am I like my Teacher? Am I being made like Him in my thinking, character, and actions?

A religious culture has taken over most churches today. We've gotten away from what it truly means to be disciples of Jesus Christ and to follow His teachings. These four steps of following Jesus are critical on the path to being a true disciple.

We leave. We learn. We love. And we lead.

Jesus called so many people who felt unqualified and far from God. Maybe you feel that way too. Still, the invitation is open. It doesn't matter who you are, where you've been, or what you've done. Jesus called Peter the fisherman, Levi the tax collector, and Mary Magdalene who had been demon possessed. He's also calling you, inviting you to draw close and learn from Him. Drop your nets and take His yoke upon you, for it is easy and light.

MAKE IT REAL

- Who was the greatest teacher you've ever had in your life? Was it a coach? A schoolteacher or a music teacher? A youth leader? What caused that person

to have such an impact on you? How are
you different because of him or her?

- Are you still clinging to things or relationships that hinder your growth as
Christ's disciple? What activities could
you limit this week that would allow you
to learn more from Jesus? He loves to be
with you.

- Do you feel Jesus' deep love for you? If
not, consider the four areas of discipleship you've just read about, and ask Jesus
to reveal where the obstacle is. Is the
issue in your past (leaving), your mind
(learning), your heart (loving), or your
actions (leading)? Take a drive, go for a
walk, or spend a moment on your knees,
and let Jesus fill you with a new sense of
His unfailing love. Commit to not only
believing in Jesus but also obeying His
commands.

4

IN THE COOL OF THE DAY

Relating to God the Father

Anyone who has seen me [Jesus]
has seen the Father.
—JOHN 14:9, NIV

I ABSOLUTELY *LOVE* BEING a dad! For real, nothing is better. I cried at the birth of all my kids, love every minute with them, and wish I could freeze-frame every glorious moment we have together. Each one of my children makes me want to hold him or her out like Mufasa held Simba during the presentation ceremony in *The Lion King*. If, like the Bible says, they are arrows in my quiver, I want to draw them back as far as the bow will allow so they can fly through the air when I release them.

I love them! I don't love them because of anything they've ever done for me but because they are mine. I want to protect, guide, and support them and see them develop and maximize their gifts and talents. I see them as Jedi Knights in training. I would give my life for any one of them. I'm also acutely aware that I often fall short as a dad, but I'm striving to be a good father because fathers are so important to the development of kids. I don't want to be a stumbling block to my own. If

I do it right, they will have a better impression of who God is.

Now, let me ask you a loaded question: What was your dad like?

Our earthly fathers have a direct impact on our views of God, and the sad truth is, countless numbers of people have difficulty relating to God the Father because of negative experiences they had with their own fathers. On the flip side, some have an easier time relating to God the Father because they had good dads. In my case, I was fortunate to have a loving dad who led by example.

Dads out there have an awesome and serious responsibility, wielding such powerful influence over their children's views of God.

Here's another question: Who is your real father?

In today's world, this can be a loaded question. Some say, "I have four dads. I have a biological dad, a stepdad, another stepdad, and another stepdad." Others say, "I don't even know my real dad. He split." Or, "My dad abused me." I don't know your particular family scenario, but the truth is, we all have two dads. We each have an earthly father who gave us our DNA. We also all have a heavenly Father, the God of the universe, who created us, breathed His life into us, and gave us a spirit. In essence, He birthed us into being.

When Adam and Eve fell in the Garden of Eden, our relationship with God the Father was broken. Sin separated us from Him. Because of this separation, we had a limited idea of what our spiritual Father was like or how to relate to Him—until Jesus stepped onto the scene. Our Father sent His Son to reveal who He is and to reconcile us to Him. "And all of this is a gift from God," wrote the apostle Paul, "who brought us back to himself through Christ. And God has given us this task of reconciling people to him. For God was in Christ, reconciling the world to himself."[1]

As mentioned earlier, Jesus is the exact, visible image of the invisible God. I like to say Jesus has a patent on God. When my brother had a son, the two of them looked identical. "That's what I want," I told myself. "I want my son to look just like me. I want him to bear my image and be in my likeness." When he popped out of the womb, I was like, "Yeah, nailed it!"

Jesus reflects His Father. It's like looking at God in a mirror. I'm not talking about His physical DNA. I'm talking about Jesus' perfect reflection of the Father's nature and character. Jesus was loving, compassionate, and merciful. He healed people's illnesses. Jesus also had a tough side. He cast out devils that tormented people. With a whip, He cleared greedy merchants and money changers out of the temple to preserve His Father's honor. Jesus didn't want His Dad misrepresented. We can look to all these things and see the heart of the Father represented in Jesus. He is merciful and loving as well as holy and just.

Some people say, "I read about God in the Old Testament, and He's brutal and harsh. Then I look at Jesus, and He's compassionate and full of grace." Yes, they may seem different, but they are not. Jesus Himself told the crowds, "If you trust me, you are trusting not only me, but also God who sent me. For when you see me, you are seeing the one who sent me."[2] The two are one and the same. Both God the Father and God the Son hate sin, which is why Jesus, in submission to His Father's plan, took all the punishment for sin upon Himself on the cross. It was an act of holiness, justice, and our Father's unfathomable love.

Most of us know our biological fathers. Some have good relationships with their dads while others resent them. But our heavenly Father loves us more than our earthly fathers ever could. When I held my little seven-and-a-half-pound baby boy a few years ago, I was filled with so much love that I felt I would explode. I just wanted to squeeze him with everything I was feeling. It's an unexplainable love, the love I have as an earthly dad. Our heavenly Father's love is even greater. It's beyond comprehension. It's supernatural. As the author of life, He put each one of us together in our mother's womb. But here's the thing. The only way to get to know your spiritual Dad is through His Son. Jesus said, "I am the way, the truth, and the life. No one comes to the Father except through Me."[3]

The Bible says that God has set eternity in the human heart.[4] This simply means our Creator, the heavenly Father, has placed something inside us that longs for eternity with Him. Many of us feel that empty hole inside. We intuitively know we are created for something more, and we are in turmoil when we don't feel close to our heavenly Dad, who breathed into us and created an eternal spirit within us. Oftentimes, relational pain and turmoil with our earthly fathers causes us to stumble in relating to God the Father. Until we reconnect with Him, we will have an unmet longing in our hearts—a longing God wants to fill. Our heavenly Father longs to meet with us in the garden, as He did with Adam and Eve, walking with us in the cool of the day.

Do you want to know your Creator better? Thankfully, it's possible to have and deepen your relationship with your heavenly Father through Jesus Christ. This is the good news of the gospel. When you come to Jesus, He says, "Now that you know Me, let me introduce you to My Father."

Then the *real* Jesus takes it a step further. He models how we are to relate to His Father.

OUR STANDARD AS BELIEVERS

I've noticed in families, especially my own, that typically the oldest child sets the trend for how the rest of the children treat the parents. If the oldest child disrespects, then the younger ones will also disrespect. If the oldest shows honor, that becomes the expectation for the others. In the kingdom of God, Jesus Christ is our eldest brother.[5] The way He relates to the Father is our standard as believers. Jesus modeled this for us in five specific ways.

Jesus honored His Father.

Honor is a lost term to a lot of our society today. We have lost sight of how to honor veterans, the elderly, and parents. We don't know how to honor our country's leaders. We are all equal as human beings created by God, but by trying to put everybody on the same level, we have lost the honor for those in hard-earned positions or places of authority. Honor means to give weight, preference, and respect to something. In the way Jesus lived His life, He showed an honor for His Father that was so important.

Some people act as though God is a big teddy bear in the sky who simply loves everybody. "Don't you know we're all going to heaven? And hey, there's no such thing as hell." The truth is, although God is love, He is also the judge of the universe. Your Father means serious business in that regard, and His absolute holiness demands our honor. When the disciples asked Jesus to teach them how to pray, Jesus replied, "Our Father in heaven, hallowed be Your name."[6] What's His name? Hallowed, which means holy, sanctified, set apart. Jesus could've said His Father's name was good or generous or wonderful, but He pointed out that it was holy. He was giving His disciples a revelation of the magnificent holiness of God.

Jesus also honored God the Father with honesty. One thing God hates is hypocrisy. We see this reflected in Jesus' life. He constantly went after the Pharisees who gave the outward appearance of being all holy and religious when in reality their hearts were deceitful, corrupt, and wicked. Inside, they were dead men's bones, and Jesus told them to their faces they were whitewashed tombs![7] The way we honor God is by coming before Him honestly and admitting we are total wrecks. Such honesty honors God.

Honesty is birthed from humility, another thing we see in the *real* Jesus. We dishonor the Father when we don't recognize we are merely dirt that He has breathed into. "For if anyone thinks himself to be something, when he is nothing," wrote Paul, "he deceives himself."[8] Do not deceive yourself. You are never going to have a strong relationship with your heavenly Father without humility. "So humble yourselves under the mighty power of God, and at the right time he will lift you up in honor. Give all your worries and cares to God, for he cares about you."9 God the Father cares for us. He wants to provide and be a part of our lives, but we must desperately depend on Him, understanding that apart from Him we are nothing and can do nothing. The very purpose of our existence is to be in fellowship with Him. Honesty, honor, and humility bring us closer to God.

Finally, we honor God with our lifestyles. People who truly love their fathers are going to live in ways that honor them. When I was growing up, my dad had a morning TV show called *Lifeline*. A brief, two-minute-long devotional, it was very popular, a kind of wake-up call people watched while getting ready for school or work. All of us kids carried Dad's likeness, and because he was a presence on television and pastor of one of the largest churches in town, we couldn't go anywhere without people saying, "Aren't you Larry Stockstill's kids?" A lot of people thought the pastor's children had to be perfect. We were far from it, but because we bore his image, we had to try. No matter where I went, if I did something mischievous, somebody would see me and say, "I know who you are. You're a Stockstill." Sometimes I was like the apostle Peter, denying it three times. "No, I'm not!"

Nowadays, our culture says we can live any way we want and God will accept it. Let me tell you, that's a lie. Yes, God loves us, but He wrote the Book. As we follow the *real* Jesus, we honor our Father with lifestyles that align with His laws.

Jesus obeyed His Father.

Our obedience to God is a direct result of our love for Him. Jesus went so far as to say that keeping God's commandments is equal to loving Him.[10] Jesus obeyed everything His Dad told Him. This isn't always easy for us, and it wasn't always easy for Jesus. When the Father wanted Jesus to die as a sacrifice for the world's sin, Jesus was in so much agony in the Garden of Gethsemane that He sweat drops of blood. This is an actual medical condition called hematidrosis,[11] brought on by extreme emotional or physical stress.

The Bible says Jesus fell with His face to the ground and cried out, "My Father, if it is possible, may this cup be taken from me. Yet not as I will, but as you will."[12] Jesus could have opted out at any moment, but He chose to obey. That is how much He loved His Father and how much He loved us. If we really love God and have His love in us, we will have a deep desire to obey what He says. If we are not seeking to be like Jesus and to align our lives with God's ways, then we are not loving Him. It's that simple.

I'm talking not about sinless perfection but about a life aimed toward obedience. You can say you love. You can say love wins. You can say whatever, but you are not filled with the love of God if you don't obey Him. If you don't want to take my word for it, check out this passage from God's Word: "If someone claims, 'I know God,' but doesn't obey God's commandments, that person is a liar and is not living in the truth. But those who obey God's word truly show how completely they love him. That is how we know we are living in him."[13]

I love my kids more than words can say. I would die for them. That doesn't mean I approve of their disobedience. Though God loves us, He still has a standard. We are all called to align ourselves with Him, and we cannot honestly say we are in right standing with Him if we ignore His Word.

Jesus loved His Father.

Obeying God is directly linked to loving Him, yet obedience is not love. Does that make sense? Think about it. If you do not obey, then you do not truly love. On the other hand, your obedience to God is a by-product of your love relationship with Him. And Jesus modeled this love for the Father. He got alone with God late at night and in the wee hours of the morning. They were one, having had a relationship of unity and love since before time began. Then, while Jesus was on the cross, He cried out, "My God, My God, why have You forsaken Me?"[14] At this point, for the first time ever, the Father withdrew and looked away from His Son as He bore the sins of the world. For Jesus, it was so emotionally painful because He had always experienced a close relationship with the Father. Out of obedience, Jesus loved His Father to the point of death.

Like Jesus, you as a Christian must *honor* your Father. You *obey* Him. And you *love* Him. Even when we feel like the Father has turned away, we know He is at work and His love never fails. Maybe your earthly father was abusive. Maybe he was not present. Maybe he wasn't there emotionally. If you've put that on your heavenly

Father, I challenge you to take another look at Him. He is fully present, the lover of your soul. He is perfect, and His love for you is perfect. He wants you to receive that love, and then you need to reciprocate that love to Him. It's the reciprocal love Jesus modeled for us as He walked the earth. "We love Him because He first loved us," the Bible tells us.[15] That's the design.

Jesus trusted His Father.

Jesus said, "It is written, 'Man shall not live by bread alone, but by every word that proceeds from the mouth of God.'"[16] He cast Himself into the care of the Father. As a Christian, you will not always have things work out right in your life. There may be some months when you don't have enough money. Trust God. Maybe you get a bad report from the doctor. Trust God. Maybe a dear loved one dies. Trust God. Maybe terrible things are happening in the nation you love so much and you don't understand what's going on. Trust God. Maybe one of your children has left or your marriage is in crisis. Trust God.

The bottom line is this: Jesus had utmost trust in the Father. If you want to relate to the Father the way Jesus did, you have to trust Him. God is sovereign. He's so much bigger than anything you will face in this life. He has it all under control. Proverbs 3:5–6 sums it up well: "Trust in the LORD with all your heart, and lean not on your own understanding; in all your ways acknowledge Him, and He shall direct your paths."

Jesus talked to His Father.

Luke 5:16 tells us, "But Jesus often withdrew to lonely places and prayed" (NIV). Sometimes that makes me scratch my head. Why did He even have to pray? Jesus was constantly praying, modeling it for us, yet we as Christians don't seem to pray very much. Prayer is so powerful. It releases God's will to be accomplished in our lives and our surroundings. Prayer is agreeing with God, and we don't agree with Him enough.

Not long ago, I was reading about Daniel. The Bible says he prayed three times a day—morning, midday, and night. He prayed constantly for *seventy years*. How do modern Christians compare? How often do we talk to the Father? How often do we spend time hanging out with God?

Beyond giving us the Lord's Prayer, Jesus modeled a lifestyle of prayer that was powered by a simple conviction: The Father saw Him. He heard Him. He knew Him. He loved Him. Jesus was confident that the Father had His back. I believe we as Christians need to be challenged to relate to God as Jesus did. We need to build a lifestyle of prayer. Seeking God should be so ingrained in us that it becomes a natural part of who we are.

If you want to relate to God the Father the way Jesus did, you need to honor Him, obey His commands, love Him with all your heart, trust Him completely, and spend time walking and talking with Him in the cool of the day because He's a good, good Father.

MAKE IT REAL

- How has your relationship with your earthly father impacted your view of Father God? Be honest, and ask God to reveal His heart for you as your heavenly Father.

- Reflect on any areas in which you have trouble trusting God—finances, family, careers, relationships. What steps of faith can you take in these areas this week?

- Block out distractions, and make an intentional effort to get alone with God. Express honor, confess areas of disobedience, and tell your Father of your love for Him.

A MAKE-IT-HAPPEN KIND OF POWER

Relating to the Holy Spirit

And I [Jesus] will ask the Father, and he will
give you another Advocate, who will never
leave you. He is the Holy Spirit, who
leads into all truth.
—JOHN 14:16–17, NLT

I REMEMBER AS A kid in Sunday school reading the
story of Samson. I imagined him like a superhero,
like Captain America—or should I say, Captain
Israel? He picked up city gates, set his enemies' fields
on fire, and fought a whole army with a donkey's jaw-
bone. He was invincible! The secret of his power was
in his hair, which seemed strange, but that's where his
vulnerability lay. I remember cringing when I heard
that Delilah deceived him, cutting his hair and causing
him to lose his power.

If the key to Samson's strength was his hair, what
was the secret behind Jesus' supernatural abilities?
Was it His divinity? What was the source of His power?

The Gospels tell us that Jesus had the Spirit without
limit and that He returned from the temptation in the

wilderness full of the Spirit's power. The Holy Spirit was His secret, the way He stayed in sync.

In today's culture, it's virtually impossible to survive without Wi-Fi. Wi-Fi connects us to the world around us through messaging, emails, and social media. It's our access to the worldwide system of information through sites such as Google and Wikipedia. It has become almost as important as electricity or air conditioning. The Holy Spirit was Jesus' connection, providing access to His Father, to His assignments, and to the power of heaven. Jesus did only what He saw His Father do first, and He could see that only because of the Holy Spirit.

Here's a question I've asked my kids: "If you had to go back in time several thousand years and could bring only one thing with you, what would it be?" They've said everything from a gun or knife to a car or plane. Once you play out all the scenarios, you realize what a difficult decision it would be. If you brought a car, you would eventually run out of gas. If you brought a gun, you'd run out of bullets. A book of ancient languages may be of some help, but who knows.

When Jesus came to earth, He basically left the most sophisticated society, the kingdom of God, and traveled into time with only one tool from that eternal realm to help Him navigate this world's craziness. That tool was His relationship with the Holy Spirit.

The Holy Spirit was all Jesus brought with Him. With the Spirit's help, He had to fulfill every prophecy. He had to live a perfect, sinless life. He couldn't afford to make even one mistake. What a challenge! Still today, the Holy Spirit is Christians' only hope of fulfilling all the things we are created to do. We need Him not only to demonstrate God's supernatural power but also to love those around us the way Jesus wants. We need the Spirit to live in obedience to God's Word, resist temptations to sin, and even keep our mouths shut when we want to lash out. It's impossible to be a true disciple of Jesus without a deep relationship with the Holy Spirit.

The Holy Spirit was everything to Jesus. Jesus guarded the Spirit's name and honor the way the Secret Service guards the president. Jesus didn't really mind if people said horrible things about Him, but He issued a serious warning to those who spoke against the Spirit: "Anyone who speaks against the Son of Man can be forgiven, but anyone who speaks against the Holy Spirit will never be forgiven, either in this world or in the world to come."[1] That's a severe judgment coming from the One who embodies grace and mercy.

Jesus' words remind me of the Yo Mama jokes I heard growing up. Guys went back and forth, each one seeing who could give the worst insults about the other's mother. They got mad and even fought over jokes about their precious moms. In the same way, Jesus absolutely did not tolerate comments made about the Holy Spirit. The purity and holiness of God's Spirit were too sacred to take lightly.

Jesus knew firsthand the power associated with the Holy Spirit. I'm not talking about atomic power or even explosions on the sun. I'm talking about universe-creating power. When God said, "Let there be,"[2] He demonstrated a make-it-happen kind of power. All that power dwelled in Jesus, ready to be unleashed with just a word. It was limitless power, able to heal the sick, drive out devils, and calm storms. It was the same power that raised the dead body of Jesus back to life. In the Greek, it is called *dunamis* power.[3] It's where we get the word *dynamite*.

The Holy Spirit was given to Jesus so He could accomplish every assignment given Him. For us to truly be Christ's followers and demonstrate the same works He did—and even greater works—we need to be empowered by the same Spirit. It is impossible for us to walk in the same anointing Jesus had without it. This is why Jesus insisted that the disciples not leave Jerusalem until they had received the promised Holy Spirit. Only after the Spirit came upon them would they receive *dunamis* power to take the gospel "to the ends of the earth."[4]

Most Christians would love to walk in the power Jesus operated in, but we often fail to acknowledge the source of His power: His intimate relationship with the Holy Spirit. I believe Jesus was in a constant dialogue with the Spirit, completely trusting the Spirit's voice and leadership. Thankfully, Jesus gave us several keys to knowing the Holy Spirit the way He did.

LET HIM EMPOWER YOU

The disciples must have wondered where Jesus derived His power. When they woke up each morning, they noticed He was already gone. He spent hours alone with His Father, and they naturally concluded this was His source of power. Why do I think that? Because they didn't ask Him how to work miracles, heal the sick, or walk on water. They asked Him to teach them how to pray! He gave them some pointers for prayer in Luke 11—persistence, privacy, and pattern. Then He finished with this important phrase: "How much more will your heavenly Father give the Holy Spirit to those who ask him!"[5]

Just as the Father gave the gift of the Spirit to the Son, He wants to give Him to us. He will absolutely fulfill that promise to anyone who requests it. If my young son asked me if he could drive a brand-new Ferrari, I wouldn't grant that request. There is so little experience on his part to go with so much power. His maturity doesn't match the privilege. Yet God knows exactly what He's doing and gives us the Holy Spirit to grow us up in God. It is truly impossible to be a Christ follower without the Spirit, and the Father stands by, ready to give Him to all who ask.

LET HIM TEACH YOU

In this day and age, we need truth in the worst sort of way. The current mantra seems to be "Don't confuse me with the facts. My mind is made up!" A lot of fake news and erroneous teaching are out there, and people just soak them up. Information is coming at us faster than ever before. In 2013, we were told human knowledge was doubling every twelve to thirteen months,[6] and now it's believed that knowledge is doubling every twelve hours.[7] I can't wrap my head around that!

The problem is, we don't need more information. What we need is more truth. And who better to reveal truth than the Spirit of truth? Jesus said, "But when he, the Spirit of truth, comes, he will guide you into all the truth. He will not speak on his own; he will speak only what he hears, and he will tell you what is yet to come."[8] The Holy Spirit authored the Scriptures. He inspired them. He illuminates and shines on them the light of understanding. This is why people who are not born again and do not have the Holy Spirit inside can read the Bible and get nothing or, worse, come up with some strange doctrine. The Holy Spirit in us is the "it" factor.

Each day when I open my Bible to study God's Word, I say, "Holy Spirit, reveal to me Your original intent when You wrote this scripture." We all need to do this, because people will come along with myriad theologies, opinions, and interpretations of Scripture. We need to seek the Author so He can explain to us the actual intent. We can know the truth. We don't have to be in the dark or be deceived. Jesus said, "And you will know the truth, and the truth will set you free."[9] The proof that something is truth is that it will set you free. If you're not walking in freedom, then you haven't taken hold of the truth.

For example, when you understand and apply the truth about God's plan for finances, you start to be free financially. When you get a hold of the truth about addiction, you begin to experience freedom from bondage that can't be taken away. Living in this freedom has everything to do with soaking ourselves in God's Word and letting the Holy Spirit help us. We may forget things we should know, "but the Helper, the Holy Spirit, whom the Father will send in My name, He will teach you all things, and bring to your remembrance all that I said to you."[10]

That's a pretty big deal, if you ask me, because I desperately need that help. I need His still, small voice to illuminate the truth, to guide and encourage me, and to give me supernatural insight about various people and situations. When you invite the Holy Spirit to work and move in your life, He'll do amazing things to bring glory to the person of Jesus.

LET HIM GUIDE YOU

My wife and I are into sailing. It's a fun and engaging pastime—we love it! During one of our first overnight trips in a sailboat, we had quite an experience. After a peaceful night's rest, we awoke early and started the twenty-mile sail back to the base marina. The skies were clear, and I did something no sailor should do. I forgot to check the weather report. About an hour later, the skies grew dark and the wind picked up. When I looked at the radar, it scared me beyond words. We were pointed directly into a squall. There was no turning around, no running for shelter. The only option was to keep moving ahead.

When the wall of wind and water hit, I was completely unprepared for the chaos that ensued. It was intense. At one point, I put on scuba goggles just to see through the blinding rain. I was supposed to be heading 270 degrees due west, but my compass told me I was headed due north. We were going to hit the shore! Thankfully, with that big, round compass in front of me, I was able to correct course even though I could hardly see.

For those of us who believe, the Holy Spirit is our compass, our GPS. As mentioned earlier, Jesus said, "He will guide you into all the truth...and he will tell you what is yet to come." When we stay close to the Spirit, He gives us turn-by-turn instructions. Sometimes they're even given minute by minute. This is exactly how Jesus operated. He woke up every morning and followed that still, small voice, being led by the sacred Spirit of God.

The early apostles did the same.

For instance, Philip was told to walk down a dirt road, and because he obeyed the Holy Spirit's direction, he ended up baptizing an Ethiopian official. Moments later, he was transported to another place! Peter was told to go to Caesarea to help out a Roman officer, and he did just that. Paul was instructed to go west instead of east, and as a result he spread the gospel in Philippi, Thessalonica, and other areas of Macedonia. Over and over we see Christ's followers being directed by spiritual GPS, namely the Holy Spirit. This is a fundamental trait for those of us who want to be disciples of Jesus. We rely on the guidance of the Holy Spirit.

LET HIM MOVE THROUGH YOU

We know this for certain: we have no natural power to do miracles. Our bodies are built to operate in this natural world, and in the flesh we will never produce supernatural results. We can strain, cry, and wait all day, but nothing will happen. On Mount Carmel, the prophets of Baal tried to prove their spiritual power over the power of Elijah's God. They cut themselves and screamed for hours to their god yet received no response.[11] Although we serve almighty God, not Baal, we can't manufacture supernatural results either. Not in our own strength. However, when we allow the Holy Spirit to flow through us with all the explosive energy that fueled creation, amazing things will happen.

This is how Jesus performed every miracle. The Holy Spirit was the agent of power behind each and every one. Every prophetic word Jesus spoke was first whispered to Him by the Holy Spirit. Every inconceivable miracle, such as calling a man who had been dead four days out of his grave,[12] was backed by the great power of God in the form of the Spirit.

If we are to do these same things, we must allow the Holy Spirit to do what only He can do. Our part is the natural; His part is the supernatural. We lay our hands on the sick; He performs the miracle. We open our mouths to speak; He gives us the words. To flow in the power of the Spirit, we must trust Him. It takes faith. Our relationship with the Holy Spirit is interdependent and symbiotic. Because we trust Him, we step out in obedience. And because we step out in obedience, He supplies the power that only He has.

Just as Jesus allowed the Holy Spirit to flow through Him, we allow God's Spirit to move through us as we grow in our relationship with Him. By Him we can speak mysteries, prophesy, minister healing, and see miracles take place. Everything the Word says we can do, we can do by the Spirit.

DO NOT LET HIM BE IGNORED

Considering how powerful the Holy Spirit is, it may seem odd that He can be quenched or grieved, but the Bible tells us this is the case. The Spirit is omnipresent and omniscient, aware of absolutely every injustice and evil transpiring at every moment in history. When He dwells inside believers, we become His temple—and God's temple should be holy and clean. In 2 Chronicles, God's glory filled Solomon's temple after its construction, and even the priests couldn't enter because of the weight of it.[13] The Holy Spirit fills our lives in this same way. He comes to make His home in us.

When Ananias lied to Peter in Acts 5, Peter told him he had not lied to man but to the Holy Spirit. The Holy Spirit was inside Peter as Ananias lied to his face. As a result of his deception, Ananias fell over dead. This is such a sobering reality. I think about it often. Everything I say, He hears. Everything I think, He knows. Everything I see, He sees. Once a believer is filled, the Holy Spirit is ever present within. The Spirit's job is to sanctify us and perfect us. He is well aware of our shortcomings and sin. He's seen it all before. I don't think our imperfections are what grieve Him. What grieves Him is when we disobey, disregard, and, even worse, ignore Him. Because He is the most precious person in our Christian faith, left to us by Jesus, to ignore and act as though He isn't is the biggest offense. He should be treasured and valued the same way Jesus valued Him. When the Holy Spirit speaks, we should stop everything and listen. When He asks us to do something, we should move heaven and earth to obey. When He finds someone who will guard His presence and live to please Him, the world will be shaken by the impact.

The person who discovers how to live and commune with the Holy Spirit discovers the very secret of Jesus' life. It is the behind-the-scenes secret to every supernatural act Jesus performed. The most beautiful part about it is that this secret is promised to each believer—if you just ask and receive.

MAKE IT REAL

- Do you ever feel out of sync, disconnected from God? Does the Bible seem dry to you at times? The Holy Spirit is a person. Commit to spending time in conversation with Him, and ask Him to illuminate God's Word and will for you.

- In what ways have you ignored the Spirit's GPS? Let Him redirect you, and learn to listen to Him throughout the day. Is there someone He wants you to talk to or pray for? Yield to His nudging today.

- If you've never welcomed the Holy Spirit into your life, find a private place, lift your hands to heaven, and say, "Holy Spirit, I yield to You. I welcome You into my life. Have Your way!"

- Step out by faith into the gifts of the Spirit. Ask Him to use you in the different varieties of gifts mentioned in Romans 12 and 1 Corinthians 12.

PART III

JESUS—LOVING LIKE HIM

6

THAT GENTLE HUMAN TOUCH

Relating With Compassion

But a Samaritan, as he traveled, came where
the man was; and when he saw him, he took
pity on him. He went to him and bandaged
his wounds, pouring on oil and wine. Then he
put the man on his own donkey, brought
him to an inn and took care of him.

—LUKE 10:33–34, NIV

AS WE LEARN what the *real* Jesus taught, we quickly come to see that our vertical relationship with God should directly affect our horizontal relationships with people. Christianity is not just about how we relate to God but about how we relate to others. The way we treat others mirrors what is going on in our own souls. If our walk with God does not touch those in our circles of influence with His love and compassion, then we must question the health of our walk. Some people think they are close to God because they go to church, yet in day-to-day life they are rude, impatient, and selfish. This ought not to be, and Jesus displayed the exact opposite. He walked and moved with compassion, and as we are conformed to His image, our lives should be marked by compassion too.

Jesus was a lover of people. He loved His creation. He smiled at humanity. He came to earth with a heart of compassion. During His formal ministry, which was basically a three-year walk to the cross, Jesus helped people from the time He woke up in the morning till He went to sleep at night. He healed them. He fed them. He gave them something to drink. He spoke life into them. Jesus never turned away the wounded and brokenhearted. It was the self-righteous, religious hypocrites whom He sternly rebuked.

Matthew writes that once, after being followed by a large crowd, Jesus healed all the sick who were present—all of them. Then Matthew quotes from Isaiah, adding a prophecy concerning Jesus: "A bruised reed he will not break, and a smoldering wick he will not snuff out."[1] John Abbott wrote in his acclaimed Bible commentary, "The *bruised reed* and *smoking flax* [wick] are emblems of helplessness, dejection, and sorrow. The images are expressive of the mildness and gentleness with which Jesus instills truth into the minds of his followers, and of the tender care which he exercises in sustaining the weak, restoring the fallen, and raising the dejected and desponding."[2]

In Luke 10:25–37, a religious expert comes to Jesus and asks what he needs to do to be saved. Jesus directs the man to what is written in the Jewish law: "'You shall love the LORD your God with all your heart, with all your soul, with all your strength, and with all your mind,' and 'your neighbor as yourself.'"[3]

Trying to justify himself and test Jesus, the guy asks, "And who is my neighbor?"

Jesus never flinches. In a genius move, He tells the parable of the good Samaritan, a story of how three people—a priest, a Levite, and a Samaritan—react to a person in need. He starts with the priest: "A certain man went down from Jerusalem to Jericho, and fell among thieves, who stripped him of his clothing, wounded him, and departed, leaving him half dead. Now by chance a certain priest came down that road. And when he saw him, he passed by on the other side."[4]

In place of *priest*, you could put *pastor*, which hits close to home for me. The story is alarming because this priest/pastor saw the injured man and moved to the other side of the road. I don't know why he didn't help. Maybe he thought the man was too far gone and there was nothing he could do. Some commentators believe the priest had just finished ministering in Jerusalem and was returning to Jericho.[5] Jericho is about fifteen to eighteen miles away, with a descent of more than three thousand feet.[6] The desert road is arid, the air is salty, and the weather is hot—crazy hot.

Sweaty and exhausted, this priest probably felt like he'd already done his spiritual duty. It's so easy to be judgmental toward him, yet I've been that man many times. I've poured myself out in ministry, felt empty, and simply passed on by when the next need appeared. It seemed like too much, just too inconvenient for me to dive in and do something. But the parable makes it clear that the priest was in the wrong, no matter his excuse. And we're all guilty of the same thing at times. We pass by on the other side.

Like many of us, the priest thought spirituality was a matter of worshipping God, reading the Scriptures, and paying his tithe. Of course, those things are important, but if our worship remains vertical and never turns horizontal, we miss the whole point. The most spiritual thing you can possibly do is love and help your neighbor.

The *real* Jesus is about helping the guy on the side of the road—yes, even before you go to church.

Jesus continues with the parable, telling about the second guy who comes along: "Likewise a Levite, when he arrived at the place, came and looked, and passed by on the other side."[7] In case you're wondering, a Levite was basically a worship leader in the temple. Uh-oh. That's me again. Before becoming a pastor, I spent years recording worship albums and leading worship around the world. And here we see the Levite did the same thing as the priest!

Then there's the third guy, a Samaritan. In Jesus' day, the Jewish people despised and looked down on Samaritans because they were of mixed heritage—half Jewish and half Gentile—and their lineage could not be traced. A Jewish person seen talking to a Samaritan was instantly rebuked and ostracized. But when a despised Samaritan entered Jesus' parable, things started to look up for the wounded traveler: "And when he [the Samaritan] saw him, he had compassion. So he went to him and bandaged his wounds, pouring on oil and wine; and he set him on his own animal, brought him to an inn, and took care of him."[8] The Samaritan even paid the innkeeper from his own pocket, promising to reimburse him for any other expenses incurred.

Isn't it great that Jesus chose a Samaritan to be the hero of the story?

Through the parable of the good Samaritan, Jesus gives us four elements of compassion.

EYES OF COMPASSION

Although the priest and the Levite both saw the half-dead man with physical eyes, they refused to really see. They did not have the Samaritan's eyes of compassion. It's possible to both see and close your eyes at the same time, but living a life of compassion requires eyes wide open to the needs around us. Jesus models this compassion for us throughout the Gospels. Seven times, we read that "Jesus saw."

- Jesus saw the spiritually hungry inquirers and invited them to join Him, and they spent the day with Him (John 1:38–40, NLT).

- Jesus saw Nathanael under the fig tree and later commended him (John 1:47–50).

- Jesus saw the man who had been sick for thirty-eight years and healed him (John 5:5–6).

- Jesus saw the hungry crowd and fed them (John 6:5–11, NLT).

- Jesus saw the blind man, then revealed Himself as the light of the world and healed him (John 9:1–7).

- Jesus saw the weeping mourners and was moved with empathy for them (John 11:33).

- Jesus saw His distraught mother, and He made sure she was taken care of (John 19:26).

In each case, Jesus was moved with compassion when He saw those in need, and He is moved with compassion when He sees you. We're talking about a Jesus who really sees—not just some situations but every situation and circumstance. He sees your problem right now, and He understands. Jesus feels your pain.

It is good to be seen, but our own needs can often eclipse the needs of others. "Hey, I'm the one on the side of the road who needs to be cared for," we cry. "Somebody, please help me!" The truth is, if you're walking through something tough, one of the greatest ways you can get out of it is by helping someone else. I can guarantee there's always somebody worse off than you, and if you want to be like Jesus, you have to lift your eyes to see the needs around you. Jesus tells us to do exactly that: "Behold, I say to you, lift up your eyes and look at the fields, for they are already white for harvest!"[9]

Many of us move at such a fast pace that everything becomes a blur. We rarely slow down long enough to see the assignments Jesus has for us, and when we do, we have so many excuses for not acting: "I don't know if I can trust that charity organization." "I'm not sure where to give my money." "I don't have the right skills to help." "I've been burned before."

I love the following poem, called "The Paradoxical Commandments," written by Dr. Kent Keith. Mother Teresa reportedly hung a version of this on the wall in her orphanage in India. Part of the poem goes like this:

> People are illogical, unreasonable, and
> self-centered.
>
> Love them anyway.
>
> If you do good, people will accuse you of selfish
> ulterior motives.
>
> Do good anyway....
>
> The good you do today will be forgotten
> tomorrow.
>
> Do good anyway....
>
> Give the world the best you have and you'll get
> kicked in the teeth.
>
> Give the world the best you have anyway.[10]

A guy once told me it bugged him that there seemed to be a homeless person asking for money at every street corner. "I have a strategy for it," he told me. "I leave a space between me and the car in front of me. When the person walks up to my car, I just pull ahead." The guy may have thought it was funny, but his actions were definitely not Jesus-like. If we're not careful, we can turn mean, judgmental, and insensitive. Indifference, like cataracts, can blind our eyes of compassion. This may be what happened to the priest and the Levite.

I challenge you now to lift your eyes. Compassion starts with what you see.

A HEART OF COMPASSION

We called my grandma Mimi. Mimi had such a big, soft heart. One day, my dad—just a kid at the time—was watching an old program like *The Andy Griffith Show* on their black-and-white TV when a drunken stranger wandered into the house. Mimi rushed into the living room the moment she heard the low, mumbling voice. She walked right up to the guy, put her hand on his chest, and marched him out the door. She slammed and locked it, then opened a window and asked the man, "Can I fix you a sandwich?"

That was Mimi. She implemented programs to feed and clothe the poor, started homes for unwed mothers, and selflessly gave to missionaries around the world. Mimi exemplified a true heart of compassion.

In the parable Jesus told, the Samaritan "felt compassion" for the injured man. The New International Version says in Luke 10:33, "When he saw him, he took pity on him." The Samaritan, moved by compassion and pity, took action. It's not enough to just see. We must also engage our hearts to do something.

Who is the most compassionate person you can think of? All of us know, or at least know of, a big-hearted person who wants to help everyone. We have a man on our church staff whose heart is so tender he cries when he sees people hurting. We kid him that he would shed tears over an Alka-Seltzer commercial. Mother Teresa gave her life to helping the suffering in Calcutta. But Jesus took compassion to a much higher level. In the Gospels, when we read that Jesus was "moved with compassion" by one thing or another, it means in the Greek that His guts hurt.[11] He was the most compassionate person who ever lived, and His compassion went from His eyes straight to His heart.

At times Jesus couldn't even walk outside because of the sick and the hurting crowded around Him. Once, an entire city gathered at His door. I can picture the disciples treating Jesus like an A-list celebrity, trying to help Him avoid the paparazzi. They might have plotted a getaway out the back. That wasn't Jesus' style, though. The Bible says, "At evening, when the sun had set, they brought to Him all who were sick and those who were demon-possessed. And the whole city was gathered together at the door. Then He healed many who were sick with various diseases, and cast out many demons."[12]

Jesus stood at the door and received those with leprosy, cancer, tumors, demons, and paralyzed limbs. He could not leave them untouched. He said, "Come to me, all of you who are weary and carry heavy burdens, and I will give you rest."[13] And Jesus loved the kids too! I bet if He were a pastor today, He would rather be a kids' or student pastor than the adult pastor. He wanted to bless the children. He turned no one away.

One day Jesus and His disciples were walking down the road when two blind men heard Him nearing. "Lord,

Son of David," they cried out, "have mercy on us!" The crowd told them to shut up, but the Bible says, "When Jesus heard them, he stopped and called, 'What do you want me to do for you?' 'Lord,' they said, 'we want to see!' Jesus felt sorry for them and touched their eyes. Instantly they could see! Then they followed him."[14]

In the village of Nain, Jesus was deeply moved by a funeral procession where a widow had lost her only son. Touching the coffin, He raised the dead boy back to life.[15] On another occasion a leper came to Him and fell on his knees, begging to be healed. This time, the very sight of the oppressive leprosy enraged Jesus, and Scripture says, "Jesus was indignant. He reached out his hand and touched the man. 'I am willing,' he said. 'Be clean!' Immediately the leprosy left him and he was cleansed."[16]

Have you ever seen a TV commercial about children starving in another nation and suddenly felt pain in your insides? Or have you seen a guy with no legs in a wheelchair pushing himself down the sidewalk in the rain and felt your heart just explode?

That's the compassion of the *real* Jesus.

We should feel deeply, as He does, about injustice. When we see or hear of unborn babies killed in the womb, sex trafficking around the globe, domestic abuse, people living in extreme poverty, and the way Satan wars against our world, it should enrage us the way leprosy enraged Jesus.

Lift your eyes.

See the needs.

Feel them deeply.

Become indignant.

The sad truth is, many of us are just plain callous. We've seen so much and laid layers of stone over our hearts. We need to say, "Jesus, take away this stony heart and put in me a beating heart of compassion that loves people as You do." Once we remove the cataracts from our eyes and the callousness from our hearts, it's time to do something about the needs around us.

A TOUCH OF COMPASSION

The Bible tells us the good Samaritan went to the injured man and attended to his wounds. At some point, Jesus' deep compassion for the lost and hurting should move us from feelings to action—even if it's just making a sandwich for someone. We can get hung up on feeling bad about different situations and yet never do anything. It happens all the time. The priest was a prime example of ignoring the need. The Levite also ignored the need. And the Samaritan could have easily justified inaction by thinking, "Neither the priest nor the Levite helped. Why should I?" He had to make a decision. He could either dive into the drama, the chaos, and inconvenience or pass on by like the other two.

It's not always convenient to be compassionate. It's easier to go on a website, click on the give button, and feel good about our good deed for the year. But life is messy. Showing true compassion may cost you time or money. It may require physical energy or mental effort. Sometimes you have to climb down into the trenches and get dirty. Being the hands and feet of Jesus to others is one of the greatest spiritual acts you can engage in.

Jesus often touched those whom He healed. He

didn't have to touch them to heal them. Jesus is God. All He had to do was say the word, and people would be healed. This happened time and time again. In the case of the leper, though, Jesus was moved deeply by the man's condition.

In those days, lepers were considered unclean and had to call out, "Unclean! Unclean!" everywhere they went. There was no cure for the contagious disease. Your family kicked you out of the house, and you went to live in a leper colony. As the deformity worsened—sometimes causing the face to look like that of a lion—your damaged nerves began to lose all feeling. If you cut yourself, infection could set in before you even realized you were injured.[17] You were miserable, an outcast.

Instead of being revolted, Jesus felt pity and sorrow for the man. He placed His hands on that disease-ravaged man and brought him close. Touch wasn't necessary for the leper's physical healing, but imagine the healing love he experienced in Jesus' gentle human touch. His condition was instantly healed. With one touch of compassion from Jesus, his life was forever changed.

There are people this very day who just need a hug or somebody to pray with them. What am I saying? Slow down enough to see the needs around you. Feel them deeply, let them sink into your heart, then allow that compassion to flow to your hands and take action. This is the Jesus way.

A WALK OF COMPASSION

When the good Samaritan chose to act, he involved all his resources and time. He didn't just bandage the injured man. He put him on the donkey he had been riding and walked alongside the rest of the way. He didn't just drop the man off at the inn. He doctored the man through the night. He covered all the expenses.

Wow. That is the walk of compassion. The lowly Samaritan, despised by others, issued a divine challenge to all of us.

Now I'm going to tell this story from a slightly different perspective.

Jesus is the good Samaritan. The man lying on the side of the road is humanity—you and me. Sin has beat us up. Sin has robbed from us. Who is the thief? Who is the robber? It's Satan. Satan comes to steal, kill, and destroy. He tries to destroy nations. He tries to destroy families. He tries to destroy individuals. He tries to destroy kids. He is the thief, and he needs to be exposed as such. God is not the thief. God is not the robber. God is not the one responsible for human suffering.

The priest who walked by represents the Law. He saw the need but was unable to meet it. Knowing the commandments and satisfying their demands will never get you healed or right with God. Religion can't save you. Going to church and obeying the Law can't save humanity.

The Levite represents the prophets. In ancient Jewish culture, they thought that following the Law and the prophets would save them, but it only pointed out their sin and guilt.[18] Jesus, however, fulfilled the Law for us. He is humanity's only hope.

Here's how Isaiah 53:3 describes Jesus: "He is despised and rejected by men, a Man of sorrows and acquainted with grief." It's no coincidence that Jesus chose the Samaritan to illustrate compassion, because Jesus was also lowly and despised. He knelt down for humanity, just as the Samaritan did for the injured man. He left the comforts of heaven and came down to earth to cleanse our wounds with His precious blood and comfort us with the oil of His Holy Spirit.

Then Jesus carried us all the way to the inn, which represents His church, His hospital. He paid the price and told the innkeeper, God the Father, He would take care of any other expenses incurred. Our past sins, present sins, and future sins—all of them are covered by Jesus' blood for those who surrender their lives to Him.

The *real* Jesus is the good Samaritan. He looked down from heaven and saw us with *eyes* of compassion. His beating *heart* felt the suffering of His creation. Then He became a man so He could *touch* us and heal us. Finally, He *walked* out His compassion by laying down His life to save ours. These four elements of compassion become manifest in us as we grow in grace and are molded and conformed to the image of Jesus. We are to be His hands and feet to a wounded and dying world.

MAKE IT REAL

- In what areas do you need Jesus' healing touch? Do you ever believe the lies that you are unclean? The good Samaritan is kneeling at your side. Tell Him honestly the places you feel inadequate or broken.

- Are you ever like the priest or the Levite, caught up in activity, too busy to help anyone else? Ask God to soften your heart and show you ways to show compassion this week.

- Think about people you pass by regularly—neighbors, coworkers, family members. Do they have needs you can help with? Consider making a lunch, sending a note, or offering to babysit. Spend time with them and lift them up.

NO FISHING ALLOWED!

Relating Through Forgiveness

Then Peter came to him and asked, "Lord,
how often should I forgive someone
who sins against me? Seven times?"
"No, not seven times," Jesus replied,
"but seventy times seven!"
—MATTHEW 18:21–22, NLT

I N OUR WORLD there are many injustices but none equivalent to the injustice brought upon Jesus by an angry mob and a cruel government. He was the unblemished Lamb, the epitome of wisdom and love. Not only had He never committed a crime; He had never even spoken a sinful word. He was perfect.

As Jesus hung on the cross, enduring the torment brought upon Him by Jewish leaders and Roman soldiers, He uttered these beautiful words: "Father, forgive them, for they do not know what they do."[1] With just one word, He could have stopped all of their heartbeats. Instead, He had compassion on them.

On a long list of things Jesus showed us about relating to people, forgiveness is right at the top. The forgiveness He taught is unique to Christianity. It's not popular in our world to forgive injustices. We seize on the Old Testament instruction to take an eye for an eye and a tooth for a tooth, but that is not the way of Jesus, who told us to turn the other cheek.[2] Jesus didn't deserve the death penalty. True justice would have been execution for all those involved in His murder. But He cried out for His Father to be merciful toward them. Mercy triumphed over judgment.[3]

Jesus exemplified this heart of forgiveness throughout His lifetime, though it was most pronounced around His crucifixion. Judas, who had been with Him for three years, sold Him out for money. Peter, His right-hand and leading apostle, disowned Him. His own nation, the focus of His entire ministry, handed Him over to the Romans.

Jesus forgave them all.

When Jesus came to Peter after the resurrection, He extended His beautiful forgiveness to the man who had purposefully denied Him. I often wonder what would have happened if Judas had stuck around after the resurrection. I personally believe Jesus would have forgiven him just as He forgave Peter. For some, that statement is jaw-dropping, but I know Jesus and His love, and He even loved Judas.

Of course, no greater case can be made concerning the forgiveness of Jesus than the fact that He forgives billions of people of billions of sins. His grace and mercy are such powerful forces.

So what does this mean for us? It means we are obligated to walk in His footsteps and example. Our Master demonstrated ultimate forgiveness toward every person who wronged Him, including you and me, and that leaves us with no option but to do the same.

What's at stake if we don't? If we don't release others from their offenses against us, it cuts us off from the forgiveness of God. Jesus said in Matthew 6:14–15, "For if you forgive men their trespasses, your heavenly Father will also forgive you. But if you do not forgive men their trespasses, neither will your Father forgive your trespasses." The cost of unforgiveness is expensive. When we don't forgive, God won't even listen to our prayers! We are doomed to spiral downward into bitterness, hatred, and death. Forgiveness is hard, but our lives depend on it.

THE ROOM CAN BE UNLOCKED

The Pharisees taught that you were supposed to forgive someone two times—three times if you were really holy.[4] Peter, the same guy who later denied Jesus and then received His forgiveness, asked, "Lord, how often should I forgive someone who sins against me?" Then to seem extra spiritual, he added, "Seven times?"

Jesus looked at him and replied, "No, not seven times, but seventy times seven!"[5] We can all do the math. Seventy times seven equals 490. And Jesus is talking about forgiving the same person that many times! Some people reading this already have friends or family pushing that line. They know someone who's at 489 right now. But by saying seventy times seven, Jesus actually meant we are to extend unlimited forgiveness.

We all have people who have wronged us numerous times. Depending on the level of offense, we might be able to forgive the first time easily, but by offense number three or four, we usually get fed up. We no longer want to talk to or be around that person.

Many of us have at least one or two people who are objects of our unforgiveness. These are the ones whose names make us change the subject. They caused us such great pain, hurting us in ways only tears and anger can express. We can forgive everyone but them. We put them in a room all by themselves, close and lock the door, and try not to think about them. Yet these are the very ones Jesus has in mind.

Forgiveness like this requires a supernatural love that is bigger than us. It is beyond our own ability to keep forgiving. None of us can give or receive unlimited grace and forgiveness unless empowered by the Holy Spirit. It has to be a God thing. But with His help, the door to that room of repeat offenders can be unlocked. The Holy Spirit can empower you to forgive them, even if they are up to offense number 491.

What does forgiveness really look like? Here are some steps Jesus taught that take us on the pathway toward forgiveness.

A DECISION IN THE HEART

Before anything comes out of your mouth, it must first happen in your heart. Jesus didn't have a personal conversation with each person who crucified Him, but He did declare to God the condition of His heart. He decided in His heart to forgive.

Decisions to forgive the *real* Jesus way have to do with understanding what forgiveness is and what it is not. The Greek word Jesus used for *forgiveness* was *aphiēmi*, a legal term meaning "to let go, give up a debt, forgive, to remit."[6] It's a lot like the definition of *forgive* in Noah Webster's 1828 *American Dictionary of the English Language*: "to pardon; to remit, as an offense or debt; to overlook an offense, and treat the offender as not guilty."[7] Just as in a court of law, the primary issue was whether a law was violated. If so, here was the penalty. Feelings didn't determine the outcome. It was a legal decision.

Forgiveness too is a legal transaction, not an emotional one. Yes, a debt is owed, but forgiveness is choosing to release the debt owed to you.

Imagine you take a person to court because he owes you a mortgage payment and won't pay up. After hearing all sides, the judge agrees with you and charges the person to pay the money. In that case, justice has been served. But what if you tell the judge, "Wait, I'm stopping this. I hold the mortgage. I know he owes me, but I've had a change of heart. I believe what I'd like to do now is just cancel his debt. I know he can't pay it, so I'll just give him the house and not worry about it. In fact, hand me a red pen if you've got one, Judge, and I'll write 'Paid in full' across the bottom."

That's what forgiveness looks like. That's *aphiēmi*. It's a decision, choosing to let go of an obligation someone else owes you. Although the decision comes from the heart, it is not based in feelings. It is an act of your will.

In fact, this is exactly how God forgave you. He *decided* to forgive you based on the merits of Jesus' blood on the cross. He paid your debt and *decided* to write at the bottom of your mortgage, "Paid in full by the blood of Jesus Christ." Check out this passage, which describes it perfectly: "When you were dead in your transgressions and the uncircumcision of your flesh, He made you alive together with Him, having forgiven us all our transgressions, *having canceled out the certificate of debt* consisting of decrees against us, which was hostile to us; and He has taken it out of the way, having nailed it to the cross."[8]

Did you know that in New Testament times, debt was canceled by driving a nail through the legal document and fixing it to the doorpost of that person's house?[9] Why do you think Jesus had nails driven through His hands and feet? Symbolically, His body became the list of our sins, of our debt. The debt was owed to God, and in one defining moment at the cross, He canceled it out forever. Because of Him, I am completely free. Some days I feel it. Some days I'm down. But no matter how I am feeling, my freedom is a legal fact.

If God did this for us, we must do the same for the people we've locked away in unforgiveness.

Maybe you're thinking, "I don't know if I can forgive." On your own, you can't. It's a supernatural thing by the enabling of the Holy Spirit. That is the only way. With the Spirit's help, what you have to do is pull out those IOUs hidden deep in your pocket. Like the one that says, "He took my girlfriend my senior year." Yep, you've still got it down on that crumpled piece of paper. That thing's about thirty years old now.

I want you to take it to the cross and nail it there. It's a decision.

And then you say, "Yes, it's painful, but it's over."

Maybe one of your neighbors lets her garbage blow over in your yard every day. Every morning you need to nail it to the cross, then go pick up the woman's trash and let God release you as you throw it away. Maybe that neighbor's getting close to 490 times, but you can still make the decision.

Years ago, my dad had the privilege of meeting Corrie ten Boom, a precious Christian woman whose family hid Jews in their home in Holland during World War II. Eventually Corrie, her sister, and their dad were arrested and thrown into Ravensbrück, a Nazi concentration camp. All three suffered separation, starvation, beatings, mental torture, and other horrendous things. Corrie's dad and sister died during the Holocaust, but because of a clerical error, she was released from the camp. During this horror beyond what most of us can fathom, God taught her about supernatural freedom from anger and fear.

After the war, Corrie traveled the world sharing her story of pain and forgiveness. One day, she was offered a speaking opportunity in Germany of all places. She met there with a church group in the basement of a home. Using the Old Testament, she told them how God forgives our sins and buries them in the depths of the sea. It's a message she shared often, telling people God then puts up a sign that reads, "No Fishing Allowed!"

After the meeting was over, a man walked up to Corrie. She sensed she had seen him before, and then it dawned on her he had been a guard at Ravensbrück prison. The memories came rushing back like a tidal wave—the shame and humiliation of stripping down with her sister and all the women in the camp and putting their clothes in a pile in the middle of that room, and this man standing before them like a vicious animal, his eyes filled with death and perversion.

As Corrie stared at him in the basement church, her mind's eye replaced his brown hat with the skull-and-crossbones cap he wore in the concentration camp. She could see the leather whip that once hung from his belt. She heard its cracking and the sounds of women screaming.

She wondered if he remembered her, if the same horrific images were flashing into his mind.

The man stuck his hand out in greeting. "A fine message, Fraulein! How good it is to know that, as you say, all our sins are at the bottom of the sea!"

No, he did not remember her.

His hand was still extended, but Corrie couldn't respond. So she began to fumble around in her purse.

"You mentioned Ravensbruck in your talk," he told her. "I was a guard there. But since that time...I have become a Christian. I know that God has forgiven me for the cruel things I did there, but I would like to hear it from your lips as well. Fraulein...will you forgive me?"

Corrie stood there for what was probably seconds but felt like hours as she wrestled with the man's request. This was the hardest thing she'd ever been asked to do. She extended her hand, woodenly, barely able to even lift it. Then something incredible happened. "The current started in my shoulder," she later wrote, "raced down my arm, sprang into our joined hands. And then this healing warmth seemed to flood my whole being, bringing tears to my eyes."

As they joined hands, forgiveness came flooding into Corrie's heart. "I had never known God's love so intensely, as I did then," she wrote. "But even so, I realized it was not my love. I had tried, and did not have the power. It was the power of the Holy Spirit."[10]

With that small act of Corrie's will, God was able to step in and give her the power she needed. If you make a decision to forgive, God will also give you the power to take the next step of having conversation.

A CONVERSATION OUT OF LOVE

I would give anything to have been a fly on the wall when Peter and Jesus had their first conversation after the resurrection. I'm sure Peter was shocked and thrilled that Jesus was alive, but it had to be a little awkward. After all, the last memory Peter had of Jesus was His eyes piercing Peter's soul after that rooster crowed the third time, fulfilling Jesus' prophecy about Peter's denial of Him. At some point, Jesus had to address the issue. Rather than ignore what had happened, He brought it up. On the beach of the Sea of Galilee, the conversation happened.

Jesus, in His most loving way, asked Peter, "Do you love Me?" He was opening the door for a much bigger conversation centered on love and commitment, not the act of betrayal. Three times Jesus asked the same question, and three times He allowed Peter to correct his mistakes by affirming his love for Christ. Jesus never brought up Peter's failure. Instead, He gave him an assignment: "Feed My sheep."[11] Jesus didn't just tell us we should forgive and leave it at that. In talking with Peter and others, He demonstrated how we are to have conversations with people who have done us wrong.

Oftentimes Christians don't deal with offenses this

way. Rather than having conversations, we go in our woundedness and talk about our pain to different people in the body of Christ, telling everyone how badly we were treated. We present one-sided stories and gather a consensus of support that makes us feel justified in our offense. Yet if we just did what Jesus said to do, we could avoid a lot of damage. He said, "Go and tell [the person] his fault between you and him alone. If he hears you, you have gained your brother."[12] The purpose of having this conversation is to gain a brother or sister, not to argue your point or to attack. Winning an argument is not winning. We win when we are reconciled. That's the power of a private appeal.

It sounds so easy on paper, but when you try it, you quickly find it's not easy at all! In fact, a lot of you would have that conversation, except you just can't pick up the phone to make the call. You can't write the email or the text. You can't knock on the door or meet face to face because you're hesitant to step over into the realm of confrontation and awkwardness. Instead, you deal with it inwardly. Here's the problem with that—the wound festers and never heals. It scabs over, and from time to time, the scab gets pricked and the poison oozes out.

Offense is a trick of Satan. He wants us to harbor bitterness down in our hearts, giving him something to work with. When we hold that bitterness within, we're the ones who become prisoners to it, not the ones who offended us. I know people who've held grudges for twenty years. Inwardly, they seethe and await their day of payback or revenge, all the while going to church with their offenders sitting in pews nearby. This kind of harboring is dangerous and threatens to destroy God's family. The apostle Paul wrote, "And when I forgive whatever needs to be forgiven, I do so with Christ's authority for your benefit, so that Satan will not outsmart us. For we are familiar with his evil schemes."[13]

Many people believe that having confrontation is not walking in love. Actually, when done with the right attitude, having confrontation and conversation is a great act of love. In fact, you can bear sin for not confronting a situation. I'll give you a scripture for that. Leviticus 19:17–18 says, "You shall not hate your brother [or sister] in your heart. You shall surely rebuke your neighbor, and not bear sin because of him. You shall not take vengeance, nor bear any grudge against the children of your people, but you shall love your neighbor as yourself: I am the LORD."

What this means is you sometimes need to have a frank conversation. Don't hate that person in your heart and let the wound fester. Begin an open dialogue to identify and remove the source of offense. Get to the point and clear the air. When you do, healing can happen. Real love is not burying an issue and refusing to deal with it. It is having that conversation, dealing with that issue, and forgiving that person who offended you. Take marriage, for example. I wouldn't want to be in a union where stuff builds up over the years and is never dealt with, because this can lead to divorce. Jesus said the Law of Moses permitted divorce because the people's hearts were hard. When you do not have conversations, hardness of heart happens from layer after layer after layer of repressed emotions. Healing starts with "Let's talk about what's going on. What are you feeling? Please forgive me." When restoration is complete, that is real love.

One of the most incredible things I've ever seen Christians do happened in Charleston, South Carolina, after a terrible incident in one of the churches there. African American believers were having a Bible study, discussing Scripture and enjoying each other's fellowship. A young man named Dylann Roof joined them, then shot down nine people in cold blood. At the time, it was the worst mass shooting in the history of the American church. It's absolutely unthinkable the level of demonic activity and hatred that filled that young man's heart. It's hard to wrap our minds around it.

It's also hard to wrap our minds around what happened a few days later.

During a bond hearing, the judge let the victims' families address the shooter via a video feed to the detention center. Nadine Collier, daughter of one of the victims, was first. Various media outlets were there, with journalists waiting for a quote. What would Nadine say? I'm sure many expected something along the lines of "How could you? I hope you rot in hell, you piece of filth! Do you know how much pain and suffering you've caused?"

But do you know what came out of Nadine's mouth while the whole world was watching? "I forgive you," she said. The reporters, as well as most of those tuned in, were stunned. She continued, "You took something very precious away from me. I will never get to talk to her ever again. I will never be able to hold her again, but I forgive you, and have mercy on your soul....You hurt me. You hurt a lot of people. If God forgives you, I forgive you."[14]

She took her seat. And then relatives of the other victims got up in front of that young man, looked into the camera, and forgave him too. Newspapers and television outlets worldwide carried "I Forgive You" in their headlines. Christianity has rarely shone as brightly as it did in Charleston, South Carolina, that day. That's the *real* Jesus way of forgiveness.

A TREE IN OUR BRAINS

Forgiveness is first making a *decision*, an act of your will. Then it's having a *conversation*. This is a necessary act of love, but this last step is going to take some time.

Forgiveness is about your memories.

People confuse forgiving and forgetting. They're not the same thing. When we forgive someone, it's a legal matter that gets nailed to the cross. No feelings are needed. Yet we still have those memories and painful feelings, just like Corrie ten Boom did when she saw her former prison guard standing there. Some of you, like Corrie, have terrible memories. You'll be doing fine, then something happens. A trigger is pushed—and boom! All the feelings come flooding back.

Dr. Caroline Leaf, a renowned Christian neuroscientist, understands the brain better than anyone I've ever known. Her research shows that when we have a traumatic experience, our brain creates a memory tree. Our brains have millions of these trees. You can actually see them with the proper neurological equipment. Hanging on each tree in the subconscious mind are all the related audio and video for that memory, as well as the emotions attached to it.[15]

Imagine you have a forest full of memories in your subconscious mind, and you've repressed all those memories and emotions. You try not to think about the negative experiences, but when something triggers them, all those raw emotions rise up again. This causes you to relive the experience as if it is currently happening. That's why a soldier who hears explosions while away at war can develop post-traumatic stress disorder and continue to suffer back home, even years later. Despite trying to stuff the memories down, the soldier can hear one loud noise and suddenly be right back in combat, full of anxiety and stress.

The only way to get rid of those trees, says Dr. Leaf, is to plant new trees next to them.[16] New memories are what you create. By God's design, the brain is eager to learn and be reshaped. Romans 12:2 challenges us to be transformed by the renewing of our minds, and the Word of God teaches us how to forgive and think differently about people. The Holy Spirit will take that act of your will and supernaturally help you create new thoughts about that person and about that thing.

Consider the biblical character Joseph. He had a lot of emotions on his memory trees. His brothers betrayed him, threw him into a cistern, and sold him into slavery, after which he was thrown into prison despite being innocent. A person gets a lot of time to think in prison. He probably sat there stewing on all of it, revisiting his trees. But somewhere along the way, Joseph decided he needed to plant some new trees. When he asked the Lord why He had allowed all this to happen, God reassured Joseph that he had been sent to save a nation and his own family from starvation and death. This revelation replaced much of the hurt and the agony of what Joseph's brothers had done to him.

When they showed up in Egypt years later and he told them who he was, Joseph wept so hard that he could be heard from far away. After their father, Jacob, died, the brothers fell on the ground before Joseph, begging him to forgive them and not repay the evil they had done. Again, Joseph wept, but then God gave him supernatural empowerment. He said to his brothers who had betrayed him in his youth, "Am I in the place of God? But as for you, you meant evil against me; but God meant it for good."[17] Joseph comforted them. His forgiveness and understanding of God's will helped him create a new tree, a new positive memory, to replace the pain that had been there.

Years earlier Joseph had established his trust in God's plan. When Joseph got out of jail and became the right hand of Pharaoh, he was given a wife, and they had a baby. You know what he said? The child's name would be Manasseh, which meant "God has made me forget all my trouble."[18] And then Joseph named his second child Ephraim, which meant "God has made me fruitful in the land of my affliction."[19]

Joseph celebrated the fact God had made his marriage fruitful and helped him forget the troubles of the past.

God later had a plan for Peter as well. After Peter's betrayal, Jesus didn't write him off. He knew Peter would soon preach on the steps of the temple, leading thousands to salvation. He knew Peter would heal the sick, raise the dead, plant churches, and write epistles. He looked at Peter with a future perspective. Through the love of Jesus, we need to see those people who hurt us the way God sees us—with eyes of hope and destiny.

Are you ready to create some new trees?

MAKE IT REAL

- Have you really accepted God's forgiveness for yourself? Do you feel legally released from sin? Talk to God about personally receiving His forgiveness.

- Once you are assured of God's forgiveness for you, think of one or two people you have locked up in unforgiveness. They are the impossible people. Can you make a decision in your heart to forgive them? Can you release them from their debt to you, nailing it to the cross and letting Jesus mark it "Paid in full"?

- Whom are you going to have a conversation with today regarding forgiveness? Move forward in both love and courage. It may be awkward, but it's not your role to control the results. It's a step of obedience to Jesus, who modeled forgiveness for us.

8

AN UPSIDE-DOWN KINGDOM

Relating by Serving

Have this attitude in yourselves which
was also in Christ Jesus, who, although
He existed in the form of God, did not
regard equality with God a thing to be
grasped, but emptied Himself, taking
the form of a bond-servant.

—Philippians 2:5–7, NASB

I F YOU HAVE never visited Masada, I highly recommend it. Masada is an ancient fortress in Israel, located on a desert plateau close to the Dead Sea. Jaw-droppingly beautiful, it's a true testament to human ingenuity. It was built as both a palace complex and a vacation home for Herod the Great, king of Judaea, just before the time of Jesus. I'll never forget walking around that historic place, mesmerized by the amount of work and excellence that went into every detail—from the aqueduct systems and the mosaics in the Roman bathhouse to the private quarters hewed into the mountainside. The place is exquisite!

Without knowing Masada's backstory, one could simply walk around, smile, and admire the beauty of it all. But after a history lesson, you realize this landmark was the source of much torment and pain. During the final battle of the First Jewish Revolt, around 960 Jewish people took refuge at the top of the plateau, trapped there by the Roman army in the valley below. Finally, after many months, the Roman army completed an earthen ramp to the top and broke through into the refuge. To their surprise, the inhabitants had taken their lives the night before, choosing death over a life of slavery to Rome.[1]

Yes, that story struck me, but not as much as another element of the experience. I asked the gentleman leading our tour, "Who built all of this?" He told me thousands of slaves were sent to build this palace/vacation home for Herod. In the arid environment, many of the slaves died after a few days of hard labor. They were discarded and replaced, their bodies thrown off the mountain and never even properly buried. So many lives were wasted so a king could have a beautiful view. Masada showcases beauty but also serves as an ominous reminder that kingdoms throughout much of history have been built upon the backs of the people.

Kings like Herod were content to let everyone serve them at any expense. Just consider Babylonian King Nebuchadnezzar, who used his servants to build the great wonders such as the Hanging Gardens for his glory and for his wife, who missed her home in Media (modern-day Iran). And conscripted laborers in India spent nearly twenty years building the Taj Mahal so that Shah Jahān, the Mughal emperor, could mourn his lost wife.[2] So much pain and sacrifice, all for the glory and pleasure of earthly kings.

And then came King Jesus. Did He ever command

His disciples to build kingdoms in His honor? Did He use them to spend years building Him a monument? No. Rather than treating them as slaves, He said things like "The Son of Man did not come to be served, but to serve, and to give His life a ransom for many."[3] And "My yoke is easy and My burden is light."[4] A king who came to serve? A king who would give His life for His people? Never in world history has there been such a king. To the Jewish people, very familiar with the cruelty and lording of Herod, the message of Jesus was shocking. It almost made it hard to believe He was a king. He was so approachable, so humble, so serving.

Jesus represented a radical leadership shift. Think about it. Jesus, God with a face, created all the emperors, kings, and pharaohs. He made King Tut and Herod and Napoleon and Alexander. He is the King of all these kings, the Ruler and Lord of the whole universe—"who alone has immortality, dwelling in unapproachable light, whom no man has seen or can see, to whom be honor and everlasting power."[5] Yet when Jesus visited the earth, He laid aside His divinity and was born in a smelly, dirty, noisy stable. His humility allowed Him to come and serve the very people He created.

Now that's upside down.

This King of kings was raised in a home without a lot of money, by an earthly father who was a common carpenter, and when Jesus left home to start His ministry, He was essentially homeless. This is absolutely flipped around! Jesus, the Creator of the universe, humbled Himself to the lowest state of humanity, and instead of demanding a massive mountainside fortress be built for Him, He chose to sleep outdoors or in others' homes. Instead of having a pyramid built for Him as a tomb, Jesus had no place even to be buried! His body was laid in Joseph of Arimathea's own tomb.

Jesus did these things upside down, but what does that mean to us?

The apostle Paul wrote, "In lowliness of mind let each esteem others better than himself. Let each of you look out not only for his own interests, but also for the interests of others. Let this mind be in you which was also in Christ Jesus."[6] Paul continued with this underlying philosophy about Jesus: "who, being in the form of God, did not consider it robbery to be equal with God, but made Himself of no reputation, taking the form of a bondservant, and coming in the likeness of men. And being found in appearance as a man, He humbled Himself and became obedient to the point of death, even the death of the cross."[7]

If anybody had the right to cling to status and enjoy privilege, it was Jesus, but He didn't do that. Instead of demanding people fill His life up, Jesus emptied Himself. Instead of making slaves work themselves to death for Him, Jesus became a slave and died in the slaves' place. He poured Himself out, even to the point of death on a cross. And that's how He has called us to serve.

Jesus' servanthood was not without reward, though. Because He served, "God also has highly exalted Him and given Him the name which is above every name, that at the name of Jesus every knee should bow, of those in heaven, and of those on earth, and of those under the earth, and that every tongue should confess that Jesus Christ is Lord, to the glory of God the

Father."[8] In other words, Nero is going to bow. King Tut is going to bow. One day, Herod the Great, Hitler— all of them are going to fall on their faces and confess that Jesus Christ is Lord.

What a powerful passage that is!

Following the *real* Jesus inevitably leads to this amazing truth about upside-down leadership: life is not about serving yourself; it's about serving others.

THE SERVING SHIFT

Jesus-style servanthood requires a perspective shift. It will lead you to disregard status and recognize there is a spot for you. It will create in you a sense of satisfaction like you've never experienced. This shift in your way of thinking has to start in your heart. Without a supernatural transformation, you'll never be able to pull it off.

From the time we are born, we live only in our own skin and have a constant bias toward self. We don't automatically think of others. We instinctively make sure our own needs are met, then we care for those who are dear to us and for the life we've built. We are naturally selfish. But one of Jesus' main messages is to serve others.

After getting married, my wife and I enjoyed five years together before having kids. Life was blissful. We traveled, ate out, and stayed up all night bingeing on Netflix shows. This was before online streaming was a thing, and we had to receive the DVDs by mail. I don't know what got into us, but one day we decided to get a dog. He was a little Maltese named Dudley. Oh, what a cute dog Dudley was—until that first night. We put him in a bathroom, laid down some soft bedding, and told him good night. I wish that were the end of it, but it was only the beginning. He yelped all that night, and the next, and the next. I realized my dreamy cocoon of self-centered living was changing, with much of my time now focused on a fluffy two-pound canine.

Then came kids. Letting the dog out to do his business was nothing compared to changing a dirty diaper! After having our first child and experiencing months of sleepless nights with a colicky baby, I realized my old life was officially over. This is the shift I'm talking about. A shift that rips you out of your self-focused and self-centered life and puts your attention on others. That takes you from being a consumer to being a server.

There are two vastly different experiences to be had in a restaurant. The experience depends on your identity. One group of people visits the restaurant to consume. They eat, drink, hang out, and then go post a review of the place. Another group goes to the restaurant daily to work. They cook the food, wait the tables, and clean. They come to serve, not to be served.

Two worlds, two ideologies, gathered in one location.

Our world is like that, with different groups of people approaching life with different mentalities. Some are there to serve; some to be served. Which side of the table are you on? Do you have a napkin on your lap or an apron around your waist?

This mentality shift will show up tangibly in your family atmosphere. Instead of being worried about your chair, your TV show, your hobbies, and your schedule, you'll prioritize others in the family and serve them.

At your workplace, people will sense you aren't trying to climb the ladder at everyone else's expense, but you want to help others excel, have opportunities, and be promoted. At your church, you won't show up ten minutes late and leave five minutes early to avoid people and responsibilities. You will show up with a heart to give and pour out. This shift will be obvious to everyone in your life, especially those closest to you.

At the end of his life, Paul told Timothy he was being poured out like a drink offering to God. I picture a glass completely emptied of water, not a drop left. This is how Paul saw his life. It is what Jesus demonstrated as well. Daily, from morning until dusk, Jesus served and thought of others. He healed their bodies, taught them truth, set them free, gave them hope, and demonstrated the shift from a king on top to a servant underneath. At the end of Jesus' life, He literally poured out every drop of blood to serve the people of the world.

THE SERVING STATUS

Status is an interesting word. Much of our culture is focused on improving one's status. Webster's defines the word as "position or rank in relation to others."[9] Whether it's our living, social, or educational status, it's all about an increase in level. Even Facebook wants to know, "What's your status?"

The reason for this obsession with increasing our status is we are programmed by society to believe status equals respect. That's why people who can't afford a really nice car will buy it anyway to try and impress others—who largely don't care. People buy houses with more square footage than they need so they can live in a specific neighborhood, all for status. They pay too much money to enroll their kids in an exclusive school to maintain their image. Then they wind up bankrupt for overextending themselves.

To follow Jesus' model is to abandon this model of living. He completely flipped the script! Jesus taught that the least among us is the greatest and that true leadership is servanthood. The more your status increases in Christianity, the more you are called to serve. As you increase, so you must also decrease.

A friend of mine pastors a church in Destin, Florida, and I sometimes envy him living there. I'm like, "Man, God really called you to Destin?" It's an amazing beach-front city on the Gulf, and God is doing a great work in my friend's church. One of his members happens to be Gov. Mike Huckabee, former presidential candidate and governor of Arkansas, now a contributor on Fox News with his own television show on TBN. Mike is a faithful Christian man who found his place of service in the church's parking-lot ministry. He rides around in his golf cart, directing cars and giving visitors rides to the building. He's not looking for the VIP treatment, the green room, and the front-row seat. He's looking for the golf cart. Visitors show up on Sunday mornings, shocked that Mike Huckabee is their chauffeur to the church building, and it gives him the greatest joy. It also allows him to share encouraging words with those riding in his cart. He's a great example of someone who has increased in public leadership yet finds extreme value in simple servanthood.

Bottom line: the greater we become, the humbler we

should become. We should be arguing over who gets to park people in the parking lot or who gets to help with chores at home or who gets to serve at the workplace. A shift has to take place in our hearts.

So who is more important: the one who sits at the table or the one who serves?

According to the *real* Jesus, the greatest should be the lowest. The leader should be a servant. Status is upside down in the kingdom of God.

THE SERVING SPOT

Servanthood has a "spot." By that I mean God equips you to serve in a way only you can. Your time in history, your family of origin, your raw talents and abilities, your personality quirks, and many other unique things about you all point toward this spot. Think about Jesus, uniquely equipped to serve the world by saving it. Nothing was unintentional about when, where, and how the Father placed Him in human history. Paul was the same way. God found in him a unique vessel that could articulate the complexities of the gospel to a multinational audience. Whether debating with kings and rulers about the faith or writing inspired scriptures in a dungeon, Paul was fashioned for a spot.

Trust me, you are too! All of your design, all of your experience, and everything about who you are now make you a unique servant who is ready to step into your spot of serving. I get it. You've probably heard something along these lines before, and you're still trying to find the ever-elusive spot.

Here are some simple truths that will help you get there.

Have a heart that is willing to fill any spot. If you're super picky about the one and only spot for you, you'll miss many opportunities to serve. You might not be uniquely qualified to serve in a soup kitchen, but if the need is there and you have the opportunity, I promise you will leave fulfilled. Don't spend forever waiting on that beautiful aha moment. Just jump in.

Along the way, be sensitive to your deep passions. We all have them. Your heart may break for prison inmates, for kids without education in other countries, for human trafficking victims, or for unwed mothers choosing whether to keep or abort a child. Whatever you feel deeply about is a flashing neon indicator that points to your spot. You might wonder and pray for years about finding your spot when you could already be serving by heeding the ever-present burden within you.

Don't assume your spot is not needed just because it doesn't already exist. Don't always expect a cleared path to it. You may have to be a trailblazer, a spot maker. As a pastor, I often hear from people about areas of ministry they wish we had. They think we should have a stronger prison ministry or a disaster relief program or something to mentor underprivileged kids, and my response is always the same: "You should start it!" They look at me with big eyes and start stammering. In their minds, they want everything already mapped out and ready for them to jump into, but things will happen only if someone becomes a spot maker. Simply put, if you don't see your spot, start your spot.

If you are feeling inspired to find or start your spot, hear me clearly.

Go for it!

If you are forever sitting on the sidelines and wondering what you can do, you'll reach the end of life filled with regret that you didn't jump into your spot. Follow these easy steps to jump in: serve anywhere, serve somewhere that fits, serve in your sweet spot—even if it means you have to start it!

THE SERVING SATISFACTION

Jesus is quoted as saying, "My nourishment comes from doing the will of God, who sent me, and from finishing his work."[10] He even refused food at the time of this statement because He was so satisfied. Here is a secret about serving. It actually makes you full. When you focus on others, serve others, give to others, there is a fulfilling joy attached to it. The Scriptures actually promise, "Those who refresh others will themselves be refreshed."[11] So many people in today's world are depressed and hopeless, yet often the only thing they are searching for is significance, meaning, a place to serve.

I'm not big on landscaping and lawn care. Some people find solace and peace as they weed the flower bed, trim the hedges, and cut grass. Not me. I have a friend who absolutely loves cutting his grass. I interrogated him on one occasion, trying to understand how anyone could like pushing a mower around a yard. After some dialogue, I realized he felt such satisfaction when he was finished and saw the stripes and crosshatched patterns in the grass that he was now addicted to yard work. The heat, sweat, and expense of energy didn't even compare to the satisfaction he got from looking back and seeing the results of his work. That's what servanthood does for us. It gives us an internal sense of satisfaction that we are designed to feel when truly fulfilling our purpose.

Adding to this satisfaction is the joy of knowing when we serve other people, we are actually serving Jesus! "I tell you the truth," Jesus said, "when you did it to one of the least of these my brothers and sisters, you were doing it to me!"[12] Every time you serve people, it's OK to imagine Jesus' face in place of theirs, because it is as if you are serving Him personally. Go visit Jesus in prison, go serve Him some soup, or go be with Him in that cancer ward. Serve Him by serving people, and let that joy overtake you!

One thing is certain: the most satisfying words you will ever hear in your lifetime are the words of Jesus saying, "Well done, my good and faithful servant."[13]

Yes, our ultimate purpose and fulfillment in life come when we serve Jesus by serving others. However, there is a catch. Here's a warning. You can't pour refreshing water out of an empty cup. Before you can pour out, your cup must be filled. To be filled up, you must learn to receive, and for a lot of folks that is a problem.

THE RECEIVING END

There is a group of people who by nature only serve and never receive. If you're in that category, you probably were thinking this chapter didn't really apply to you—until now. You may be a mother with a special-needs child and all you do is serve. Your life is dedicated to others. Or you may be someone caring for elderly parents who can never repay that kindness. In our society, many people selflessly give their lives to serving others.

So how does this message apply to you?

Think of Peter in the Bible, so focused on serving Jesus that when Jesus knelt down to wash Peter's feet with water and a servant's cloth, Peter was appalled. Jesus wanted to wash the feet of a dirty fisherman? No, Peter wouldn't allow it! This wasn't something King Herod or King Tut or the Queen of Sheba would have ever done, and Jesus was the Christ. Peter was too proud to receive such treatment from Him.

I probably would be too. If Jesus came up to me and wanted to wash my feet, I'd be overwhelmed. I'd say, "Jesus, You're the Creator. You laid out the universe. You designed every atom and molecule. You are God. You died for me. You're holy. I'm just a sinful man! Please, I should be washing Your feet."

When Peter said similar words, Jesus looked sharply at him and said, "If I do not wash you, you have no part with Me."[14] In other words, if you don't allow Me to serve you, then you are not acknowledging Me as King of the upside-down kingdom.

That shifted Peter's priorities! "Lord, not my feet only," he said, "but also my hands and my head!"[15]

Part of serving is receiving the servanthood of Jesus and the servanthood of others. As humbling as it is, if Jesus doesn't wash and cleanse you with His blood, you don't have a place in heaven. You have to allow Jesus Christ to serve you and save you. Otherwise, there is no hope. And that is the gospel. The King of kings wants to get down on His knees. He wants to serve you, and He wants to save you. Then He wants to transform you into a servant too.

Shift your *perspective*. Disregard your *status*. Find your *spot* and your *fulfillment* through servanthood, then *receive* all Jesus has for you.

MAKE IT REAL

- In what ways do you find yourself focused on status in our culture? Does your pursuit of these things bring you comfort or stress?

- Have you found your serving spot? If you're not sure what it is, write down five things you feel passionate about. These are good indicators of where to serve.

- Meet with a local pastor or Christian leader, and share your desire to serve. There may be opportunities also at your school or your job. Be open to any spot God opens up. And always be willing to start a spot of your own!

PART IV

JESUS—LEADING LIKE HIM

9

A TOUGH PILL TO SWALLOW

Relating to the Kingdom

Seek the Kingdom of God above all else,
and live righteously, and he will give
you everything you need.
—MATTHEW 6:33, NLT

I'LL NEVER FORGET when the New Orleans Saints won the Super Bowl. I can tell you everything about that night—who was at the party, what food we ate, and who screamed the loudest when the game was finally over. It was the Saints' first time to win the Super Bowl, and our reaction proved it. We went wild! Some of the guys ran around the living room, some jumped up and down, others high-fived and screamed in each other's faces. Popcorn flew everywhere, and furniture was knocked over. This was a party. The Saints were our team, and we had a sense of pride that they had struggled all the way to that great moment and emerged victorious.

This is how many people feel about things they are a part of. You see this across the nation when one of our citizens wins an Olympic gold medal or our team wins the World Cup. The individual or team victory represents a victory for the whole nation, creating a collective sense of pride.

This same passion plays out in our patriotism. We are intricately connected to our nation. Its laws, culture, values, and ethics are meant to represent all of us, and in many ways they determine our anxiety or well-being. Rarely will citizens travel from their own nation to another to join in riots or political uprisings. They may be sympathetic to a cause, but their own lives and families are not drastically affected. We care more about our own nation and its leadership because these directly impact us.

Israel was the same way at the time of Christ. Historically, the Jewish people carried a great amount of passion for their nation, but at that time they were under Roman rule. Nobody wanted the occupiers around, and many had opinions on the matter. Tax collectors made it their business to ensure everyone paid the right amount to Rome. The Jewish Sanhedrin and religious leaders sometimes curried personal and public favors from Roman officials. The Zealots were a group that believed in fighting Rome at all costs, even when the odds were stacked massively against them. The Essenes community just wanted to be left alone in their wilderness exile. Jesus was alive at an extremely tense moment in Jewish history.

From every side, He was pressed to give opinions about the Jewish and Roman tension. Did He favor partnering with the Romans, like some of the pragmatic religious leaders? Or did He want to start a war, like the Zealots? People asked Jesus questions about taxes and whether it was right to pay them to Caesar.

They urged Him to be their king, believing He would lead them into triumphant battle against the Romans.

Jesus always responded so brilliantly, seeming to avoid the questions and often turning them back around. It was hard to pin Him down to specific opinions on these matters.

Jesus was passionate about something else—another kingdom.

Most of us think Jesus came and introduced the world to the religion of Christianity. But He actually never preached on the subject of Christianity. He preached about the kingdom of God. While the people of His day were focused on earthly governments, Jesus spoke of a heavenly one.

If you study the Gospels, you'll find this was Jesus' main message. It was His disciples' main message too. They didn't preach the religion of Christianity; they preached the kingdom of God. It was a new government active on the earth. To be more theologically accurate, it was the reestablishment of God's reign on earth. It was a kingdom similar in many ways to a human kingdom. It had a leader, laws, a culture, values, and ethics. It even had a military, an economy, and other facets that kingdoms share.

Yet it was superior in every way.

The *real* Jesus was the King of this kingdom. He was not a mortal, earthly king but the eternal, not-of-this-world King. To love Him was to give your allegiance to the kingdom of God, tearing down any competing loyalties or passions.

In the same way I'm a proud American and New Orleans Saints fan, Jesus was an extreme patriot for

His Father's kingdom. After Jesus finished mentoring His disciples, they shared His passion for and commitment to this new kingdom. His message was so strong and compelling that people came into His kingdom by the thousands. "Seek the Kingdom of God above all else," Jesus encouraged them, "and live righteously, and he will give you everything you need."[1]

Jesus had always been King of the heavenly kingdom, and now He was bringing it back to earth. It was time to restore what Adam lost in the Garden of Eden when he committed treason by disobeying God's command. All along this was God's hope and plan—to walk with His people, to move in power and love. Jesus demonstrated this kingdom power by healing the sick, raising the dead, and later rising from the dead Himself. He invited people to be citizens of this kingdom, and many of His famed parables were about the kingdom of God.

Where does this leave us today? Many of us see Christianity as a religion, and this is where we miss it big time. All our earthly nations and kingdoms are temporary while God's kingdom is eternal. Isaiah said the government would be upon His shoulders,[2] and God has a government all set up. King Jesus invites us to come alongside Him—to be citizens and rulers with Him. He wants us to replace our current passions with a passion for the kingdom of God.

This is a tough pill for many people to swallow. In America, patriotism runs deep. Many of us have loyalties within us from the time we're little kids. I grew up reciting the Pledge of Allegiance in school. I love my state's college and professional sports teams. Like loyal citizens in other nations of the world, many Americans would die for their country. Most of these loyalties are not bad things. There is a problem, though, if they are more important to us than the kingdom of God.

The Jews in the time of Christ struggled with similar things. But just as Abraham was looking for a city whose builder and maker was God,[3] we must be willing to forsake everything for the higher reality of God's kingdom.

Where do you stand? Do your love and loyalty for the kingdom of God transcend your love for all earthly kingdoms? There are three stages of putting God's kingdom first in our lives.

IDENTIFY YOUR PASSIONS

King David prayed, "Search me, O God, and know my heart; test me and know my anxious thoughts. Point out anything in me that offends you, and lead me along the path of everlasting life."[4] David asked God to look at all his thoughts and affections and to point out anything that was offensive. We must do the same. All of us have deep affections that need to bow to the importance of God's kingdom. John wrote, "For the world offers only a craving for physical pleasure, a craving for everything we see, and pride in our achievements and possessions. These are not from the Father, but are from this world."[5]

Some of us revere success. We wake up each morning and think about how we can win. Life is one big competition. We want the top sales award, the valedictorian status, the highest grade in the class, the nicest house in the neighborhood. Success is what holds the greatest value and gets our loyalty.

Some of us value attention, money, kids, or politics. None of these are sinful on their own. It's good to discover our gifts and callings and to set goals in life. God has a purpose for each of us to fulfill, a purpose that brings joy and satisfaction. But we can't let these things become idols in our hearts. If we love Jesus, we will begin to love the things He loves. That includes His kingdom, the kingdom of God.

Are you wondering what you're most passionate about? I have a quick test to help you figure it out. Answer three simple questions:

- What do you talk about the most?

- What do you think about the most?

- Where do you spend your extra income?

These three questions will show you where your heart lies.

People talk about what excites them. We all know the ones who will bring up certain topics if given enough time. Even if they mask their passions for a few minutes, we know it won't last for long. The topic may be sports, their children, a hobby, or politics, but they will talk about it. We are all like this to some degree. Jesus said it like this: "Out of the abundance of the heart his mouth speaks."[6] Boy, isn't that the truth? What do you talk about the most?

As humans, we also think about our passions. If our minds are left idle for a few minutes, they will retrieve those subjects and dwell on them. They will put our passions up on the big screen, like putting on a favorite show in your living room. What you think about the most will reveal your greatest passions.

The final test is a little tougher to discern, but your greatest passion will get the surplus of your resources. If you have some extra income, it will usually go where your loyalties lie. It may go to the deer camp, the wardrobe, or the boat. Or it may fall into a vast category of hobbies, vacations, or gadgets. When Jesus instructed the rich young ruler to sell everything, give it to the poor, then come follow Him, He was pinpointing the man's value system. If the man really valued the kingdom of God at the highest level in his life, he would have obeyed.

The three little questions we just looked at can expose the deepest parts of your heart. What do you care about the most? What has your attention?

Jesus wants it to be His kingdom.

PULL DOWN YOUR IDOLS

Once you've identified where your true loyalties lie, it's time to make some changes. In biblical terms, we would call this pulling down idols. Idols are physical statues and symbols that represent deities. It's still common practice in many parts of the world to worship statues and symbols in place of various deities. Some religions believe the deities will come and inhabit the statues. In Western culture, however, idols are almost completely a thing of the past—at least in physical form. We now look to other things such as money, sex, government, and technology to bring fulfillment, provision, and satisfaction.

Jesus wants us to pull down these idols, these passions that supersede our passion for His kingdom. But how do you change something you've cared about for so long? I gave you three questions to reveal where your heart lies, and here are three corollary tips for change:

- You have to filter what you imagine.

- You need to change what you ingest.

- You must redirect what you invest.

On paper, these tips look short and manageable, even easy. In reality, they're tough.

To change what you think about involves your willpower. Earlier, I described your thoughts as a show you put up on your big screen. Your mind is only reflecting what you allow it to play. It reveals the deeper reality of your soul. The discipline to tell yourself what you're going to think about is a skill every person should learn. If you are cutting sugar out of your diet, you choose to pass up the cookie jar even though you really want that cookie. You can tell your mind what to think about and what not to think about. You can change the internal programming and decide to think about the kingdom of God. As Jesus said in the Sermon on the Mount, we will make the kingdom of God our primary concern.[7]

A large part of controlling our thoughts is controlling what we *ingest*. I don't mean what we physically eat. I mean the diet of the mind, the realm of our thoughts. What our minds ingest will naturally become what we think about.

I love fishing. I also love boating. If I ingest large quantities of YouTube videos about fishing, you can guess what I'll think about more often. I went through a season when I was into kayak fishing—the combination of both my passions. I watched YouTube videos about it. I read articles. I followed other kayak fishermen on social media, ingesting a ton about it. After engrossing myself in the kayak-fishing world for hours and hours, it was all I thought about. I'd be trying to write a sermon and just want to go fishing. I would be in an important meeting, look at the nice weather out the window, and dream about catching fish from a boat.

For me, fishing was the passion. For others it's cooking shows. For others it's sports.

Some people ingest just the news. They watch and read horrible story after horrible story. No wonder that becomes all they want to talk about.

What you ingest you'll be passionate about. If you don't like your diet, change it.

Another way to change what you're passionate about is to change where you *invest* your resources. In J. R. R. Tolkien's *The Hobbit*, Smaug is a dragon that sits on the treasure of Lonely Mountain. He conquers the kingdom of dwarves that dwelled in the mountain and then lies and sleeps on his pile of plundered gold for 171 years. If you've never read the book or watched the movie, you should. It's a great picture of the hearts of humanity holding on to their treasure. The moment Bilbo Baggins, the hero of the story, messes with Smaug's gold, the dragon awakens and goes into a rage to guard his hoard.

The point is this: we sit on our treasure. The scripture

rings true, saying wherever our treasure is, our heart is also.[8] The two are intricately connected and codependent. If you shift your treasure, your heart will follow, and if you shift your heart, your treasure will follow. If you're having a tough time dethroning the passions and loyalties of your heart, try shifting your treasure to something else. Your heart is sure to tag along. If you give the tithe to God, watch what it does to your heart. If you give an offering to world missions and help plant a church in another nation, watch what it does to your heart. If you sponsor a kid or dig a well or go on a mission trip, your heart will be changed. Shift your treasure; shift your heart.

REPLACE THE OLD WITH THE NEW

If you're still with me, I hope you've identified your current passions and decided to change. The best way to permanently change out an old passion is to replace it with the right one. I'm talking about passion for God's kingdom.

The kingdom of God was Jesus' core message. He spoke of a kingdom that has always been, a kingdom currently among us, though invisible, and a kingdom still to come. A kingdom is simply the domain of a king, and Jesus' kingdom has been around since before the creation of the universe. Earth was an extension of His kingdom, stewarded by Adam until the fall. Now Jesus has brought the kingdom back. When He says we are to seek first His kingdom, He wants us to be inquisitive and passionate and search it out.

His kingdom is here now. It is among us.

Though unseen by the world, the kingdom is present within Jesus' followers. I am under the domain of Christ, and even though I'm walking around in this natural world as a citizen of the United States of America, I am more deeply connected to and concerned about the kingdom within. This kingdom in me is producing righteousness, peace, and joy in the Holy Spirit. It is producing in me a different and far greater culture than the one I physically live in.

The great news and hope for all Christians is that this kingdom is also coming. We need our imaginations to comprehend a kingdom that predates this universe. We rely on faith to recognize the current invisible kingdom living within us. There is a day ahead, though, when the kingdom will also be visible and all-powerful, when all earthly kingdoms will fade away and only the kingdom of God will remain. A perfect kingdom with a perfect King in a perfect future—I can't wait for that day!

If our passion is truly seeking His kingdom, we will talk about it, think about it, and invest in it.

MAKE IT REAL

- Has politics divided you and other Christians recently? Remember we are still part of the same eternal kingdom. Ask the Lord to remind you daily of who our true King is and how He wants you to interact with fellow citizens of His kingdom.

- While you were reading this chapter, did God prompt you to pull down any idols

in your heart or home? If so, don't pro-
crastinate. Respond to His still, small
voice. Family, food, and finances are all
daily concerns. Seek God's wisdom in
discerning and balancing what is sin and
what is responsibility.

10

PASSING THE TEST

Relating to Stewardship

Each one's work will become clear; for the
Day will declare it, because it will be revealed
by fire; and the fire will test each one's work,
of what sort it is. If anyone's work which he
has built on it endures, he will receive
a reward. If anyone's work is burned, he
will suffer loss; but he himself will be
saved, yet so as through fire.

—1 CORINTHIANS 3:13–15

A FEW YEARS BACK, some guys and I felt the call of the wild. We wanted to get back to nature and be pioneer men. We envisioned *Lord of the Rings*–type scenery and adventure, catching and cooking our food each day, kayaking down wilderness rivers—you get the drift. Over the ensuing weeks, we created text threads for miles about what we should do, eat, drink, and wear and all the miscellaneous details of a trip of this nature. It was incredible.

Finally, after months of planning, the day of departure was at hand. As we assembled for our big adventure, it was obvious we had all focused on different things during the preparation stages. Each guy's value system affected the way he prepared.

Some thought the only thing that mattered was food. Several guys packed big boxes of snack cakes and similar stuff. To them, it was all about going out on the river and eating snacks. Other guys thought only about fishing. They brought poles and tackle boxes—tons of tackle boxes. And for some guys, it was all about electronics so they could avoid boredom at night. One guy had a DVD player. Another guy set up Wi-Fi in his tent. He even had LED lights bumping to his Bluetooth music! The funny thing is, the same guy forgot about drinking water, and for three days we had to share ours with him. He had his tent pumping with music—but no water. He just had a different value system.

Another friend went on the trip all prepared to fish. We were pioneer men, remember? Our whole goal was to catch fish and eat the fish. He brought only one bait, though, which he lost in the first thirty minutes. Then for the rest of the trip he kept asking, "Hey, man, can I borrow your bait?"

At least it was just bait he neglected. Some guys didn't really think about bringing flotation devices. For them, that just wasn't a big deal. When we first arrived, we decided to float down the river to our campsite. Two of the guys got into a kayak, and about a half mile downriver, their kayak started sinking lower and lower. All of a sudden, they went under. That's when they realized they had forgotten to put the plugs in the bottom of the kayak! As a result, everything they brought on the trip got soaked. That night, with temperatures in the midthirties, they shivered under damp blankets in a wet tent.

Whether we realize it or not, all of us are preparing in some way for the imminent day of judgment—every single one of us. It's inescapable. One day you *will* stand before God. It doesn't matter how shy, rich, nice, mean, or popular you are. You *are* going to stand before God, and it will be all about you and Him—not your grandmother and Him, not your parents and Him, just you and Him. There will be nowhere to hide.

Whatever value systems you're using in preparation for that big day are going to show up then. Are you going to be out of fresh water? Is your kayak going to sink?

The Bible makes it very clear that one day every one of us will stand before God and our works will be tested by fire. Some of our works will be burned up like wood, hay, and stubble. It will be those things of no lasting value that for some reason seemed so important—like snack cakes and bumping music. We may bring them to heaven thinking they're great, but they'll just get incinerated. Our souls will be saved if we have committed our lives to Christ, but we will experience much loss. Some of our works, however, will be tried by the fire and come out as pure gold. This will be our treasure and what the rewards we receive in heaven are based on.

The *real* Jesus had a lot to say on this matter of preparation. He talked about getting ready for that day. He told us to prepare because it would be a day of accountability. Although judgment was one of Jesus' main themes, many people today try to ignore it. They run away from thoughts of accountability and reward. I'm convinced that besides John 3:16, society's favorite Bible verse is "Judge not, that you be not judged."[1] We don't want anybody judging us or holding us accountable.

The truth is, life is full of choices and consequences. One day, God will call us to account for the choices we made and the ways we stewarded our time, talents, and resources. It will be our final test.

Back in high school, I had a teacher I'll call Ms. Davis. She was a precious lady, and she was a pushover. Her exterior was mean, but inside she was sweet as candy.

"All right, everybody," she would say. "Pop quiz today."

Everyone sat down, but I definitely didn't know enough answers to pass. I'd mosey up to her desk and say, "Ms. Davis, you look wonderful today. Where did you get that necklace? It looks so nice on you. I don't know the answer to number two."

She'd say, "It's C."

I'd go back to my desk, write down C, and then get to number five. I really didn't know that one either. Back to her desk I went. "Ms. Davis, did you get some new perfume? It smells amazing. I don't know the answer to number five."

She'd give it to me in her steady tone.

Inevitably, I would get an A on the quiz. I'm so thankful she helped me with those tests. I would study for her class but not like I did for those teachers who I knew would show no leniency.

In God's Word, Jesus not only told us there will be a final test, but He also told us what will be on the test. We don't have to show up unprepared. He's our Rabbi, our Teacher. He may seem stern at times—and He is toward sin—but His heart is full of grace. He's given us the answers. How cool is that?

This means, however, that we will have no excuse when we stand before God. I want to be careful here. I'm not talking about a performance-based or works-based salvation. We are saved by faith alone in Jesus' work on the cross. Getting to heaven is not based on your works or personal goodness. It is Jesus' grace that saves us. The Bible clearly says, "For by grace you have been saved through faith, and that not of yourselves; it is the gift of God, not of works, lest anyone should boast."[2]

We can't skip over the next verse, though. It says, "For we are His workmanship, created in Christ Jesus for good works, which God prepared beforehand that we should walk in them."[3]

We are saved by grace.

And we are created for good works.

These good works are faith works—works accomplished as a result of who we are in Jesus. This is where stewardship becomes so important. What do we do with the assignments and opportunities God gives us? How do we use the gifts He gives us?

A friend of mine defines intelligence as being able to identify the salient issue in any circumstance. I like that. What does life boil down to? What matters most? As we prepare for our eternal test, we need to know what the salient issues of life are according to Jesus. Like Ms. Davis giving me answers to the test, Jesus clearly spells out the things on which we will be judged. So how do we get an A? How do we ensure our works will be of value and not burn up?

Jesus uses three parables in Matthew 25 to sum up life's salient issues as our *faith*, our *gifts*, and our *love*. They are ours to give away. They are ours to steward. I want to go over them with you because they are in the answers to our test.

KEEP THE FAITH BURNING

Growing up as the son of a pastor and as a pastor now myself, I've seen families come and go. Thousands of people have come through our fellowship and community of faith in the last thirty-plus years. Naturally, some move on to other cities and states. The thing that really breaks my heart, though, is when I see a family serve God faithfully for years and then back out all of a sudden. Something happens. One of them falls into an affair or gets offended by someone in the church, and they begin to pull away. Later, you hear their marriage is broken and their grown kids are not following Jesus.

I've seen it happen again and again. Christians serve God for a decade or more and then just disappear. "Where did they go?" I ask myself. "What happened to them?" Some go to other churches or ministries, and that's cool, but many, for a variety of reasons, are not following Jesus any longer. What makes someone serve God for years and then abandon Christ, abandon his or her faith, abandon His people?

Jesus said, "Blessed are those who have not seen and yet have believed."[4] When we get to heaven, every single thing we do based upon our faith in Jesus will be rewarded. The times we serve others, face persecution, make life-altering decisions, decide to live a certain way because we believe in Jesus—they will be rewarded. God won't forget even the smallest detail. If we give even a cup of cold water in His name, there will be a reward.[5] Little stories of when we chose faith over doubt will echo in eternity.

For this reason, we should always cast doubt aside. We should live like young children in a state of wonder and belief. Doubt is like gravity, trying to pull us downward every waking moment. Every time we expect God to do something and He doesn't, that gravity tugs at us. Every time we pray something and hear that whisper in our ear saying God doesn't hear, that doubt pulls us down. Every time we are disappointed, every time life doesn't go our way, every time we hear someone talk about the lunacy of faith in God, the doubt tugs at us. Faith is an upward climb. It is a mountain. We must put one foot in front of the other, always looking upward, walking against the gravity of doubt and reaching toward the pinnacle of eternity.

It is vital that we guard our faith and feed it with God's promises. All too easily doubt can creep in and extinguish the fire of faith. We see an example of this in the first parable from Matthew 25. Jesus tells a story of ten bridesmaids waiting for a groom to take them to a wedding. Each one of them has an oil lamp, but only five have enough oil to last them through the night. As the hours pass, the bridesmaids wonder if the groom is ever going to arrive. Has he forgotten them? The five maids whose lamps are burning out try to borrow oil from the others, but they are denied. When they leave to buy replenishing oil, the groom returns. He takes along the five who were prepared and leaves the others behind.

The Bible tells us that without faith, it is impossible to please God. The five bridesmaids had given up hope, and their faith grew dim. At that late hour they weren't even certain the groom would return. Their doubts and lack of planning left them empty in the end.

For Jesus, faith is a huge issue. A simple study of the Gospels shows the many times He mentioned faith. When He worked miracles, He told the recipients it was according to their faith. When He rebuked the disciples, often it was for their lack of faith. It matters to God what you believe, how secure that belief is, and how enduring it is. It matters a lot!

I pray your faith is strengthened as you read this. Don't allow the cold wind of this world to blow out the flame of faith. Don't let the long dark night find you without oil in your lamp.

This parable gives us the first answer to the eternal test: faith.

DON'T BURY YOUR GIFTS

In the next parable in Matthew 25, Jesus tells of a rich man about to go away on a journey. The man gathers three servants and entrusts some silver to each of them, according to their abilities. The first guy is given five bags, the second receives two, and the third gets one. The rich man instructs them to invest his money until he comes back. When at last he returns, he calls his servants to give an account of their silver. The first guy has worked hard and multiplied his five bags into ten.

The second servant has also multiplied what was given him, turning two bags into four. Then the rich man asks the third servant what he has done with his bag of silver. Sheepishly, the man admits he buried it in the ground to keep it safe. The day of judgment has come to the household. And what is the result?

The rich man calls the first two servants good and faithful. He gives them promotions. He celebrates them. But he calls the third man wicked and lazy. Why hasn't the servant put the silver in the bank and earned some interest at least? The rich man casts him out of the household.

I want to point out here that judgment is not always a bad thing. We typically think about judgment with negative connotations. Judgment is actually neutral. It can lead to favorable or unfavorable verdicts. For the guys who multiplied their silver, judgment was a great day. It was reward day. For the third guy, it was much tougher. His fear and insecurities kept him from trying to do even a little something with what he'd been given.

I don't presume to know all about God's judgment and how He will grade what we've done with our gifts. But clearly, it is serious business to God whether or not we are discovering, developing, and using our gifts. When He created you, He didn't just give you flesh and blood and brains. He gave you gifts, natural aptitudes, and abilities. These are your talents, your treasures. God gave them to you to use. He has invested in you and expects a return not only of interest but also of multiplication.

"When someone has been given much," Jesus said, "much will be required in return; and when someone has been entrusted with much, even more will be required."[6] When we stand before God on judgment day, there will be an accounting of everything He has deposited in us. And don't think He will be lax in His judgment. God is an accountant who cares about every detail concerning what's been invested in us. He expects a return.

Part of stewardship is diligently seeking to know why God created you, what makes you unique, and what makes you tick. You need to know what treasure your Creator put inside you so you can give it to Him to use. This is why each of us should pray, "God, help me to discover and apply my gifts."

We also have a very real enemy who wants to keep us bound in insecurity and fear. He wants us to think our gifts are not good enough to put out there. He wants us to keep them buried. But I'm telling you right now not to believe the lies.

God deposited His good stuff in you. What happened?

Some have the ability to write, but they're insecure about it and won't write. God's going to say, "I invested that in you." Some have the ability to lead, and God's going to say, "How did you lead?" Some are gifted speakers, and others are good at administration. God's going to say, "What did you do with that?" There's going to be an accounting for everything He's placed in your life. If you are married, this includes your spouse. God placed your spouse in your life for you to love, honor, and cherish. You'll give an account of how you handled that relationship and how you raised your kids.

There's going to be a sum total in accounting for everything we have. That's why we say, "Help us, God.

Help us to live wisely and steward our gifts. Help us to live smart, because there is an imminent day of accountability."

This gives us the second answer for the test: gifts.

REACHING OUT IN LOVE

The third story Jesus tells in Matthew 25 is one of the most sobering texts in the Bible, the parable of the sheep and the goats. It's like Jesus is giving us fair warning, and this passage is on my heart a lot. I can't get away from it. If I've read it once, I've read it a thousand times. Something about it is so gripping, so convicting, so real.

Jesus describes the day of reckoning, with everyone being divided to one side or the other. He compares it to a shepherd dividing the goats from a flock of sheep, setting the sheep at his right hand while herding the goats to the left. The sheep are those people who reached out to help the needy, the imprisoned, the naked, the hungry, and the stranger. For this, they are welcomed and rewarded. The goats are those who did the exact opposite, turning a blind eye and a deaf ear. As a result, they are sent away to face punishment.

But when did they turn a blind eye? When did they ignore the needy? Jesus explains that doing anything in His name—whether it's giving people a cup of water, visiting them in prison, or bringing them into our home—is the same as doing it to Him. When we don't do anything to help, it's as though we have deliberately rejected Him.

What's obvious to me is that how we loved others

will be one of the great tests of eternity. I often imagine myself in this story. I picture Jesus walking through a crowd of people, pushing some to His right and some to His left. Then He comes to me, as He did in the night vision I shared early in this book. Does He push me to the right or to the left?

I believe with all my heart that He will push me to the right, among those bound for eternity with Him. I believe this because He loves me, and I love Him and have made Him my Lord.

Perfect love casts out all fear.[7]

This parable brings up a huge question, though. Are we saved by doing good things for needy people? Is that how it works? A balanced look at all the scriptures pertaining to salvation would say no. I think what Jesus is saying here is that if you truly trust in God and you love Him, His love will tangibly flow through you to others. You will have deep compassion. You will respond to the needy. Your love for others will be a true indicator of your genuine faith.

Paul wrote, "God's love has been poured out into our hearts through the Holy Spirit, who has been given to us."[8] Think of that. God not only loved us, but He also poured His love into us through the Holy Spirit. We are like banks in which God has invested His love. He isn't just throwing His love away, tossing it in a black hole. Like any investor, He wants a return on His investment and expects it to multiply. He loves us so that His love can flow through us to others.

Are you feeling any conviction in your heart right now? Don't fear. We all fall short of God's glory at times. But every moment you breathe is an opportunity to change. If you feel like your life has been extremely self-focused, join the club. We all start there, but we shouldn't end there. The key is to be rooted in the love of Jesus. The rest will happen naturally. As you abide in Him, He will produce a deep compassion in you. This fits well with the third answer on our test: love.

THE JUDGE WHO HANGS THE STARS

A few years ago, I was driving home with my five-year-old daughter when she asked, "Dad, how long is this road?" I didn't know how to answer that, so I just ignored it. She wasn't done, though. She started firing off a bunch of questions, one after another like a machine gun, and I ignored all of them. Then she said, and I'll never forget it, "Dad, I'm smarter than you."

"OK," I shot back. "What's your Social Security number? Who was the second president of the United States? Who is the mayor of this city? Who is the governor of this state? What is the closest star to the planet Earth?"

She didn't know the answers, of course, and she just giggled and giggled.

After about twenty questions, I said, "Who's smarter, Daddy or you?"

And she said, "Daddy, you're much smarter than me."

There's a passage in the Bible where Job goes on and on, questioning God. Why this and why that? For a while God just listens. And I'm sure Job probably thought he was pretty smart. Then God says, "Why do you talk without knowing what you're talking about? Pull yourself together, Job! Up on your feet! Stand tall! I have some questions for you."[9]

God goes on to ask Job who created the earth. Who directs the wind and corrals the oceans? Who hangs the stars? There's not much left to say after that. It's pretty clear that our heavenly Daddy is much smarter.

Many of us, when we ponder God's judgment, think, "Man, this is intense! Should God really be sentencing some people to eternal punishment and others to eternal life? What qualifies Him to make such drastic judgments? What if He doesn't know all the facts? What if I'm on the wrong side of that judgment? Whom could I even appeal to if His judgments aren't fair?" These are all questions that run through our minds. But I know this: if anyone can be trusted with the judgment of every human being, it's Jesus—God in the flesh, God with a face, the One who created us and died for us. You can trust your life in His hands.

I've heard it said, "All my eggs are in one basket, the one Jesus is carrying." You can trust Jesus with full fairness and full justice. We should all be thankful the gavel is in the hands of a perfectly just and fair God who has been tempted and tested in every way that we have and who empathizes with our humanity. "He knows our frame," wrote the psalmist, and "remembers that we are dust."[10] No, we are not in the hands of a flawed, sinful human or in the hands of our adversary the devil. We are in the hands of the One who hangs the stars.

So why did I write this chapter? Because the *real* Jesus taught us to prepare for that day. He gave us the answers to the test. If we are born again, we do not have to be afraid. We can face God with confidence that our kayak won't sink, so to speak. Through Jesus, we can guard our faith, multiply the things He has entrusted to us, and freely give to others the love He has given to us. You're going to be OK. I'm going to be OK. There's no need to fear the day of judgment.

I think the apostle John said it best: "There is no fear in love; but perfect love casts out fear, because fear involves torment. But he who fears has not been made perfect in love."[11]

MAKE IT REAL

- Do you struggle with doubt? You're not alone. Share your struggles with a fellow believer, and be honest with God about how you're feeling. Also consider reading a biography about a great man or woman of faith such as George Müller or Maria Woodworth-Etter. This will help build your faith.

- How can you use your gifts at home, school, work, or church? Watch God multiply them as you step out in faith.

- How do you treat the poor, immigrants, minorities, and strangers in your community? Do you see them as Jesus does? Do you respond to them more like the sheep or the goats in Jesus' parable?

11

SEEK AND SAVE

Relating to Your Mission

Follow Me [Jesus], and I will make
you become fishers of men.
—MATTHEW 4:19

DURING THE 2008 Olympics in Beijing, the USA men's 400-meter relay team was favored to win. They faced some stiff competition, but many expected them to bring home the gold. First, though, they had to win their preliminary round.

On a rain-slick track, the runners took their positions. The starter's gun went off, and the leadoff American runner rocketed around the first hundred meters. He handed off the baton to the second runner, who shot down the straightaway and handed off to Darvis Patton. Less than twenty seconds had passed, and this race was already halfway over. Patton's legs were flying as he took the lead around the final turn. Now all he needed to do was pass the baton cleanly to Tyson Gay, the defending world champion in both the 100 and 200 meters. Ten more seconds and this race was theirs!

Tyson took off, stretching back his arm for the baton. As he neared the end of the exchange zone, he closed

144

his hand on thin air. Somewhere in the exchange, the baton dropped to the ground. The agony on Tyson's face confirmed that his worst nightmare had occurred. His eyes seemed to say, "This can't be happening! Not in the Olympics. We've spent years preparing for this. I've just messed up and let my team and country down!"

In that moment, it didn't matter how fast he was. It was a team sport. At the moment the exchange failed, it was over. Instant disqualification. No gold. No glory.

Christianity is all about the relay. We're a team, we're in it to win, and we still have a ways to go. Jesus was our leadoff runner. And man, did He sprint! In thirty-three short years He radically changed history, and before He ascended to heaven, He carried out His Father's plan by passing the baton to His disciples. They passed it to their generation. And each generation since has handed it off to the next.

The baton represents Jesus' mission. What is that mission? Speaking of Himself, Jesus made this clear: "For the Son of Man has come to seek and to save that which was lost."[1] When He first called the disciples from their nets and their tables, He didn't say, "Follow Me, and I'm going to make you successful and fulfill your lifelong dreams." He said, "Follow Me, and I will make you fishers of men."[2] He was passionate about saving people.

And now it's our turn. It's time to make the exchange.

Much of the *real* Jesus way is about watching how He lived, then taking the baton from Him and running our race. Are we securely grasping that mission? Or are we dropping it? If we want to carry on what Jesus started, there are three parts of the relay we must get right.

WATCH THE RHYTHM

Before the start of a relay race, each receiving runner makes a mark on the track, usually with tape. When the incoming runner's foot hits that mark, the receiver explodes forward while reaching back with an open hand. The timing must be perfect, and if he's not watching, he won't know when to wrap his fingers around the baton. In the bungled exchange between Darvis Patton and Tyson Gay, Tyson's hand closed on nothing at all.

What is the receiving runner watching for? He's calculating the other runner's speed, evaluating the rhythm of those churning legs. It's all about rhythm, and the rhythm of Jesus is *seek and save...seek and save...seek and save.* One leg is *seek*, the other is *save*, and the two never stop. We're watching Him, watching His mission. How many of us did Jesus have to seek out and save? He's after every man, woman, and child who is lost. And that is His rhythm.

Seek and save...seek and save...seek and save. Jesus is doing this all over the world, and He wants to do it through you. The apostle Paul said it this way: "God, who brought us back to himself through Christ...has given us this task of reconciling people to him....We are Christ's ambassadors; God is making his appeal through us. We speak for Christ when we plead, 'Come back to God!'"[3] Throughout the Gospels Jesus seeks and saves one person after another. The rhythm is clear.

At the same time, He demonstrates His love for

individuals. His legs may be doing the running, but His arms are in rhythm too, reaching out and drawing in. The Christian world today tends to focus on large numbers and big events. Those are great. As a pastor, I get excited about seeing thousands of people come to Jesus. Yet Jesus got just as excited about the *ones* as He did the multitudes. The ultimate Good Shepherd, He never hesitated to leave the ninety-nine sheep and seek out that single individual who was lost. Jesus is hung up on the *ones*, and we should be too.

Take Nicodemus, for example. The man had serious questions about the faith, and Jesus set time aside just to be with him. Think of it—the King of the universe took the time to converse with just one person. And the words are now known all around the world. Jesus told Nicodemus, "Most assuredly, I say to you, unless one is born again, he cannot see the kingdom of God."[4] That was Jesus' message. He didn't talk to Nicodemus about current events or sports or the weather. Jesus taught him to be born again. "For God so loved the world," Jesus continued, "that He gave His only begotten Son, that whoever believes in Him should not perish but have everlasting life."[5]

On another occasion, Jesus went to a man beside a pool of water. This man had been sick for thirty-eight years and had no way of seeking Jesus out, but Jesus went to him. The Bible says there were five covered porches at the pool, all loaded with sick, lame, and blind people. It was said that when the waters stirred, an angel was present, and healing was available for those who could get into the water. This poor man, though, was unable to move himself, and everyone else passed him by. But not Jesus. Jesus knew the man's pain and disappointment, and He intentionally sought him out to heal him. In the midst of the crowd, He saw the *one*![6]

Jesus even crossed the Sea of Galilee just to find a demon-possessed man living in the caves. After He set the man free, Jesus headed back in His boat.[7] The whole trip was for one guy.

Do you see Jesus' passion for reaching that one person who's in need?

And He's running toward us, baton in hand, asking that we run in rhythm with Him.

Our church once held a neighborhood outreach, and we met a lady who hadn't been out of her house in months. She was elderly and bound within her four walls by a severe phobia. She was unable to manicure her yard, which was a huge eyesore. The grass was a couple feet high, and the bushes and trees were overgrown. Our team cleaned up her entire yard, cutting the grass, trimming trees, and making minor repairs. While they worked, she kept coming out on the porch to see what in the world was going on. She couldn't believe that we saw her need and that we cared for her. We were able to tell her about Jesus. We were doing this because He loved her. She mattered.

Often, we give ourselves so much credit for finding God or being good, but we must remember that He loved us before we ever loved Him. He looked through all of time and saw you. He saw your helpless state. Born in a cursed world to a fallen family, you were helpless. No matter how self-righteous you may feel, you must recognize that God saw you; He came to you; He lifted you from the pit you were in. Maybe as you read this, you feel trapped in your life, like the man beside the pool or the woman locked away in her home. Know that Jesus is coming to you. He sees you, and He is seeking you out to save you.

I often laugh at how Jesus' disciples took so long to learn His rhythm. I don't know why it amuses me. Maybe it's because I see myself in their insensitivity. They tried sending away hungry crowds, but Jesus wanted to feed them. They got mad and urged Jesus to call down fire on the heads of whole communities, but Jesus rebuked His disciples for their attitude. They even tried to keep little kids from coming around Jesus, considering them an intrusion!

Seek and save...seek and save.

As much as they were around Him, they still couldn't see His rhythm. I think we often miss it too. We get caught up in our own lives, in our activities at church and the world of Christianity, and we miss the heart of the *real* Jesus. He wants to rescue people.

It's almost impossible to truly comprehend the length and depth and height of the love of Christ. Our minds can't even come close. If we want to take hold of that baton and run with it, we have to watch Jesus running in His beautiful, rhythmic stride. He is getting closer and closer, about to reach that mark we put down.

RECEIVE THE BATON

And then the moment comes! You burst ahead, gaining speed. You're stride for stride now, in sync with Jesus. Your arm is stretched back, your hand is open, and you're ready to receive the baton. There it is! It's time to take hold of it!

The baton represents three things we are receiving from Jesus—His mission, His authority, and His Spirit. They are all being passed to us.

We've already discussed His mission, but Jesus is also delegating His authority. One day, Jesus called together His twelve disciples and gave them power and authority to cast out all demons and heal all diseases. Then He sent them out to tell everyone about the kingdom of God and to heal the sick.[8] In the same way, Jesus delegates authority to us as believers. Sounds crazy, right? Like, could I ever heal the sick? Could I ever cast out devils? Jesus said, "All authority in heaven and on earth has been given to me. Therefore go and make disciples of all nations."[9] And later, "As the Father has sent me, I am sending you."[10] Jesus hands us the authority, but we have to receive the baton and run with it. When we get a revelation of the authority that Jesus is placing in our hands, we will begin to do those supernatural works.

Delegated authority is so important to understand. When I was growing up, we had quite a few different babysitters. Since there were so many of us Stockstill kids, sitters usually passed on the opportunity to deal with us. The ones who went one round with us didn't step back in the ring for round two. I admit, we could be a little mischievous and rambunctious. But when a babysitter was brave enough to take on the challenge, my parents were clear with us: they were delegating all their authority to the babysitter in their absence. We were to obey, help, and respect the sitter. We nodded our heads, but the truth was, if we caught wind that our sitters were insecure in their authority, we ran right over them. We knew quickly whether or not they had confidence in their authority.

Jesus gives us authority to tread upon serpents and scorpions. When He says that, He means we are carrying His authority over spiritual darkness. Whatever we bind is bound. Whatever we loose is loosed. But like my babysitters growing up, many of us don't fully grasp that authority. We must grab the baton and run with confidence, or the enemy is going to run over us. We need to speak to sickness, disease, darkness, and death and exercise His authority to have victory.

Although we have received Jesus' mission and authority, we cannot forget His Spirit. This is the most important gift we receive from Him.

Before Elijah went to heaven, his protégé Elisha had one request. Elisha wanted to receive a double portion of his mentor's spirit. As the story goes, a whirlwind from God came and picked up Elijah. As Elijah went to heaven, he dropped his cloak and Elisha grabbed it. He took his mentor's cloak, struck the Jordan River, and it split apart.[11] From that point on, Elisha had a double portion of Elijah's spirit on him. The Bible records that Elijah performed eight miracles and Elisha performed sixteen, exactly double.[12]

Jesus said to us, "Whoever believes in me...will do even greater things than these, because I am going to the Father."[13] As Jesus ascended to heaven, He lifted His hands and blessed His disciples, telling them to go and reach the world. But it wasn't the spirit of Elijah that He passed down. Jesus passed down His Spirit, the Spirit of God. He told His disciples, "Do not leave

Jerusalem until the Father sends you the gift he promised [the Holy Spirit]."[14] In the second chapter of Acts, the Holy Spirit fell on those who had gathered after Jesus' ascension. The Holy Spirit falls on believers today and is available to every one of us for empowerment.

You have the baton. It's time to run!

RUN!

One of the most painful things to see in the Olympics is a blunder of some kind—a false start, a trip up, a hurdle knocked over, a dropped baton. To see someone train for so long, get to the event, and lose it all because of a small error is almost too much to watch. The USA men's relay team isn't the only team that has squandered their moment. In fact, the USA women's team did the same thing in Beijing that year. But one mistake does not have to write your history. Usain Bolt also ran in those Olympics and shattered the world record for the 100-meter dash. The remarkable thing was that he did so with his shoes untied. Things could have played out very differently. Imagine if he had tripped before crossing the finish line.

We are like those athletes. We have a moment in time to run, and Jesus has already run His leg of the race. Other generations have run before us, fighting the good fight and finishing the race. Some have even given their lives as martyrs. They are that great cloud of witnesses that the writer of Hebrews talks about, and they are in the grandstands to cheer us on. I'm a third-generation pastor, but I can trace my genealogy and find many people who dedicated their lives to the service of Jesus. I know my dad's parents, Roy and Ruth Stockstill, are in the grandstands. My mom's parents, Jim and Pat Clark, are up there too with all the church fathers from centuries of church history. They are all cheering me on, cheering you on, cheering us on.

Now it's our turn to run.

Will we stay on our feet? Will we keep hold of the baton? Will we run with all our might, completing what Jesus started?

Some of us are out there running casually, like the race is a jog in the park. Some of us are fiddling with the baton instead of securing it in our hands. Many believers are running with untied shoelaces, and some don't make it to the finish line. The untied laces can be habits we don't shake, too many hobbies, vices we don't deal with. Don't let this be you. Tie your shoelaces. Deal with the things that would distract you, tempt you, or take you out of the race.

Others of us wear out. Let's face it. The Christian life is usually less of a sprint and more of a marathon. You may end up running with the baton of Jesus for decades. Passion and enthusiasm are great, but you will also need endurance. I've seen many start like a flash, sprinting with everything they have, only to drop out of the race a few months later. Long-distance running requires a pace that can be sustained for a long time.

To make it all the way to the finish, you need to stay energized and hydrated. Stay rooted in the Word of God and in your relationship with Jesus. And cling to the Holy Spirit. This will give you a fresh wind to finish the race. "Remain in me, and I will remain in you," Jesus said. "For a branch cannot produce fruit if it is severed from the vine, and you cannot be fruitful unless you remain in me."[15]

The race is on. Cross that finish line, and receive the prize! The apostle Paul said, "Don't you realize that in a race everyone runs, but only one person gets the prize? So run to win!"[16]

MAKE IT REAL

- Have you dropped the baton recently in any way? Don't let yourself wallow in self-pity. What can you do to pick things up again and finish what you started?

- How do you feel about receiving Jesus' mission? Do you feel unqualified or powerless? Start by ministering to one person. Seek out someone you know who needs to experience Jesus' love, and focus on showing it to him or her in practical ways.

- Are you distracted in the race of life? Are you worn out, ready to give up? Decide today that you will finish. Say no to any hindrances. Imagine that great cloud of witnesses, perhaps even friends or family members, and be encouraged that you are not alone.

CONCLUSION

CAN YOU HEAR THE SOUND?

Relating to the Real Jesus

And then I heard every creature in heaven
and on earth and under the earth and in
the sea. They sang: "Blessing and honor
and glory and power belong to the one
sitting on the throne and to the
Lamb forever and ever."
—Revelation 5:13, nlt

L ET ME PAINT a picture of our future. There will be a moment when all of us will take a knee, possibly even fall on our faces, before Jesus, the King of kings. I can imagine a sea of billions of redeemed humans surrounding the throne of God. There will be no need for a song leader or a preacher because we will be looking at the King with our own eyes. We will hear the deafening roar of angels singing hallelujah and the saints shouting with joy and gratitude. Jesus, the brilliant light, will shine in the center of it all. Can you hear the sound? Can you feel the power of this moment?

There will also be a moment when you meet Him face to face. He's going to look in your eyes and no one else's. He's going to call your name. You will have time to talk with Him as one talks to a friend. He will know everything about you before you even open your mouth. You will feel the most incredible love you've ever known. For those who put their trust in Him now and believe in Him though they've never seen Him, this will be the most significant and fulfilling moment they've ever experienced. To meet our Creator, to feel His love and acceptance, and to know we get to be with Him forever will be the pinnacle of existence.

Now, let me rewind to the present. Here we are in this bleak and fallen world. All around us are troubles, tension, and trauma. By faith, we must put this glorious Jesus at the center of our current lives. Yes, He will be the center of creation's worship on that day in our future, but He must also be the center of your life now.

Recently, I had a late-night chat with my two oldest girls. The lights were out, and we were just discussing life, family, and God. As we talked and laughed, we reached a moment I'll probably never forget. It got quiet for a few moments, and then I broke the silence. "Girls, if you only remember one thing, just one thing, that Dad wants you to know, it's this: Put your eyes on Jesus Christ, and never look away. No matter what happens in this life, we will be with each other in eternity if you just never look away." Of all the things their mother and I teach them, that statement is the *one* thing I would not want them to miss.

Jesus is our only hope.

He is our hope for this life and the next.

This book is my best attempt at summarizing the teachings and overall message of Jesus Christ. But all the head knowledge in the world means nothing if you don't know Him personally. The Book of John says, "And this is the way to have eternal life—to know you, the only true God, and Jesus Christ, the one you sent to earth."[1] The way to eternal life is not knowing all His teachings; it's knowing Him. Paul said that he considered everything worthless when compared with the infinite value of knowing Christ Jesus his Lord.[2] You must pursue a relationship with Him.

Most of the things I've discussed in this book happen naturally in my life as I stay connected to Christ. His Spirit inside me is showing me how to relate to the Trinity. He is helping me have compassion, forgive people, and serve others. I find it easy to think about His kingdom, the stewardship of my gifts, and the mission He passed to us. The *real* Jesus is someone you discover as you are in a relationship with Him. I'm convinced that for those who are born again and stay connected to Jesus, all the things found in this book will become a natural part of their identity. Right before Jesus ascended, He said, "When the Spirit of truth comes, he will guide you into all truth. He will not speak on his own but will tell you what he has heard. He will tell you about the future."[3]

My encouragement to you as you conclude this book is the same encouragement I gave my girls. Put your eyes on Jesus, and never look away. Make Him the center of your life, marriage, family, and career. One day, when we are together around His throne, you will know that making Him the central focus of your life was worth it. He is the pearl of great price. He's worth selling everything to obtain. And on that same day, you will understand that in Jesus' mind, you were the pearl of great price. He gave up all of heaven to come and find you. To Him, you were worth selling everything to obtain. This is *the real Jesus*. Feel His deep love for you, and then reflect that love back to Him by giving Him your all.

NOTES

INTRODUCTION

1. Philippians 3:8, NLT, emphasis added.

CHAPTER 1

1. See Hebrews 7:25.
2. See John 3:16–21 and 1 John 2:2.
3. "International Day for the Unreached," Wycliffe, accessed December 22, 2020, https://www.wycliffe.org/unreached.
4. Tom Wright, "The Resurrection Was as Shocking Then as It Is Now," *The Guardian*, August 3, 2009, https://www.theguardian.com/commentisfree/belief/2009/aug/03/christianity-resurrection-religion.
5. Isaiah 53:2, NLT.
6. *Merriam-Webster*, s.v. "anno Domini," accessed December 23, 2020, https://www.merriam-webster.com/dictionary/anno%20Domini.
7. Matthew 16:13–14.
8. Matthew 16:15, emphasis added.
9. See Ephesians 2:10.

CHAPTER 2

1. John 8:12.
2. John 14:6.
3. John 11:25.
4. Matthew 28:18, NLT.
5. See John 8:56–58.
6. Exodus 3:14.
7. See John 5:22.
8. See 2 Peter 2:4 and Jude 6.

9. Joe Rhodes, "Carson's Code," *New York Times*, January 30, 2005, https://www.nytimes.com/2005/01/30/arts/television/carsons-code.html.

10. See John 10:30–33, NLT.

11. John 10:33, NLT.

12. John 4:10, 13–14, NLT.

13. Peter W. Stoner, "The Christ of Prophecy," in *Science Speaks* (Chicago: Moody Press, 1952; online edition, 2002), http://sciencespeaks.dstoner.net/Christ_of_Prophecy.html#c9.

14. Toshiko Kaneda and Carl Haub, "How Many People Have Ever Lived on Earth?," Population Reference Bureau, January 23, 2020, https://www.prb.org/howmanypeoplehaveeverlivedonearth/.

15. W. R. Miller, Earle A. Rowell, and Philip Schaff, comps., "Skeptics for the Christian Faith," *Classic Works of Apologetics*, accessed December 24, 2020, https://classicapologetics.com/special/skepfor.htm.

16. S. Lewis Johnson, "The Word of God: The Ages Past," SLJ Institute, accessed December 24, 2020, https://sljinstitute.net/gospel-of-john/the-word-of-god/.

17. C. S. Lewis, *Mere Christianity* (New York: Touchstone/Simon & Schuster, 1996), 55–56.

18. Josh McDowell, *More Than a Carpenter* (Carol Stream, IL: Tyndale, 1977/2004), 30–31.

19. Bill Johnson, *Jesus Christ Is Perfect Theology* (Shippensburg, PA: Destiny Image, 2016), 7.

CHAPTER 3

1. See Revelation 1:17.

2. See Acts 22:3 and Acts 5:34–39.

3. Ray Vander Laan, "Rabbi and Talmidim," *That the World May Know*, accessed December 26, 2020, https://www.thattheworldmayknow.com/rabbi-and-talmidim.

4. See Luke 19:39.

5. See John 3:1–2.

6. See Matthew 4:18–20.

7. See Matthew 9:9; Mark 2:14; and Luke 5:27.

8. See Mark 8:34–38 and Revelation 22:17.
9. Luke 9:60, NLT.
10. Luke 9:61–62, NLT.
11. Matthew 8:19–20, NIV.
12. Matthew 19:16–21.
13. See Matthew 10:37; 19:29; and Luke 14:26.
14. Matthew 11:28–29, NLT.
15. Vander Laan, "Rabbi and Talmidim."
16. Matthew 11:29, NLT.
17. See 1 Corinthians 2:16.
18. See Matthew 6:25–31.
19. John 15:15, NLT.
20. John 13:35, NLT.
21. See Luke 10:27.
22. John 15:13.
23. See Matthew 10:1.
24. John 14:12.
25. Luke 6:40.

CHAPTER 4

1. 2 Corinthians 5:18–19, NLT.
2. John 12:44–45, NLT.
3. John 14:6.
4. See Ecclesiastes 3:11.
5. See Romans 8:29.
6. Matthew 6:9.
7. See Matthew 23:13–28.
8. Galatians 6:3.
9. 1 Peter 5:6–7, NLT.
10. See John 14:15.
11. Valencia Higuera, "Hematidrosis: Is Sweating Blood Real?," Healthline, March 14, 2017, https://www.healthline.com/health/hematidrosis.
12. Matthew 26:39, NIV.
13. 1 John 2:4–5, NLT.
14. Mark 15:34.
15. 1 John 4:19.

16. Matthew 4:4.

CHAPTER 5

1. Matthew 12:32, NLT.
2. See Genesis 1.
3. Bible Hub, s.v. "*dunamis*," accessed December 27, 2020, https://biblehub.com/greek/1411.htm.
4. Acts 1:8, NLT.
5. Luke 11:13.
6. David Russell Schilling, "Knowledge Doubling Every 12 Months, Soon to Be Every 12 Hours," Industry Tap, April 19, 2013, https://www.industrytap.com/knowledge-doubling-every-12-months-soon-to-be-every-12-hours/3950.
7. Scott Sorokin, "Thriving in a World of 'Knowledge Half-Life,'" IDG Communications, Inc., April 5, 2019, https://www.cio.com/article/3387637/thriving-in-a-world-of-knowledge-half-life.html.
8. John 16:13, NIV.
9. John 8:32, NLT.
10. John 14:26.
11. See 1 Kings 18:28–29.
12. See John 11.
13. See 2 Chronicles 7:2.

CHAPTER 6

1. Matthew 12:15–20, NIV.
2. John S. C. Abbott and Jacob Abbott, "Commentary on Matthew 12:20," *Abbott's Illustrated New Testament*, 1878, https://www.studylight.org/commentaries/ain/matthew-12.html.
3. Luke 10:27.
4. Luke 10:29–31.
5. Bible Hub, "Commentaries: Luke 10:31," accessed December 27, 2020, https://biblehub.com/commentaries/luke/10-31.htm.
6. "From Jerusalem to Jericho," American Bible Society Resources, accessed December 27, 2020, https://

bibleresources.americanbible.org/resource/from-jerusalem-to-jericho.

7. Luke 10:32.

8. Luke 10:33–34.

9. John 4:35.

10. Kent M. Keith, "The Paradoxical Commandments," The Prayer Foundation, 2001, https://www.prayerfoundation.org/mother_teresa_do_it_anyway.htm.

11. Thaddeus Williams, "The Emotions of Jesus, Part 3: Compassion," The Good Book Blog, Biola University, June 15, 2015, https://www.biola.edu/blogs/good-book-blog/2015/the-emotions-of-jesus-part-3-compassion.

12. Mark 1:32–34.

13. Matthew 11:28, NLT.

14. Matthew 20:30–34, NLT.

15. See Luke 7:11–15.

16. Mark 1:41–42, NIV.

17. Alan L. Gillen, "Biblical Leprosy: Shedding Light on the Disease That Shuns," Answers in Genesis, June 10, 2007, https://answersingenesis.org/biology/disease/biblical-leprosy-shedding-light-on-the-disease-that-shuns/.

18. See Romans 3:19–20.

CHAPTER 7

1. Luke 23:24.

2. See Exodus 21:23–25 and Matthew 5:38–42.

3. See James 2:13.

4. J. Dwight Pentecost, The Parables of Jesus: Lessons in Life from the Master Teacher (Grand Rapids, MI: Kregel, 1982), 61, https://www.google.com/books/edition/The_Parables_of_Jesus/k_VVxjLkN2UC.

5. Matthew 18:21–22, NLT.

6. Blue Letter Bible, s.v. "aphiēmi," accessed December 30, 2020, https://www.blueletterbible.org/lang/Lexicon/Lexicon.cfm?strongs=G863&t=KJV.

7. American Dictionary of the English Language, s.v. "forgive," accessed December 30, 2020, http://webstersdictionary1828.com/Dictionary/forgive.

8. Colossians 2:13–14, NASB, emphasis added.

9. Albert Barnes, "Commentary on Colossians 2:14," *Barnes' Notes on the Whole Bible*, 1870, https://www.studylight. org/commentaries/bnb/colossians-2.html; see also Joseph S. Exell, "Commentary on Colossians 2:14," *The Biblical Illustrator*, 1905–1909, https://www.studylight.org/ commentaries/tbi/colossians-2.html.

10. Corrie ten Boom, *Tramp for the Lord* (New York: Jove Books, 1978), 53–55.

11. See John 21:15–18.

12. Matthew 18:15.

13. 2 Corinthians 2:10–11, NLT.

14. Elahe Izadi, "The Powerful Words of Forgiveness Delivered to Dylann Roof by Victims' Relatives," *Washington Post*, June 19, 2015, https://www.washingtonpost.com/news/post-nation/wp/2015/06/19/hate-wont-win-the-powerful-words-delivered-to-dylann-roof-by-victims-relatives/.

15. Caroline Leaf, "How to Deal With Trauma, and Overcome Toxic Thoughts and Memories," May 9, 2018, video, https://www.youtube.com/watch?v=iUSIEHfQmns; see also Caroline Leaf, *Switch On Your Brain: The Key to Peak Happiness, Thinking, and Health* (Grand Rapids, MI: Baker, 2013), 151–161.

16. Leaf, *Switch On Your Brain*, 151–161.

17. Genesis 50:19–20.

18. Genesis 41:51, NASB.

19. Genesis 41:52, NASB.

CHAPTER 8

1. "Masada," History, March 4, 2019, https://www.history.com/ topics/ancient-middle-east/masada.

2. "Taj Mahal," World Heritage Centre, UNESCO, accessed December 30, 2020, https://whc.unesco.org/en/list/252.

3. Mark 10:45.

4. Matthew 11:30.

5. 1 Timothy 6:16.

6. Philippians 2:3–5.

7. Philippians 2:6–8.

8. Philippians 2:9–11.
9. *Merriam-Webster*, s.v. "status," accessed December 30, 2020, https://www.merriam-webster.com/dictionary/status.
10. John 4:34, NLT.
11. Proverbs 11:25, NLT.
12. Matthew 25:40, NLT.
13. Matthew 25:21, NLT.
14. John 13:8.
15. John 13:9.

CHAPTER 9

1. Matthew 6:33, NLT.
2. See Isaiah 9:6.
3. See Hebrews 11:10.
4. Psalm 139:23–24, NLT.
5. 1 John 2:16, NLT.
6. Luke 6:45.
7. See Matthew 6:33.
8. See Matthew 6:21.

CHAPTER 10

1. Matthew 7:1.
2. Ephesians 2:8–9.
3. Ephesians 2:10.
4. John 20:29.
5. See Matthew 25:31–46 and Mark 9:41.
6. Luke 12:48, NLT.
7. See 1 John 4:18.
8. Romans 5:5, NIV.
9. Job 38:2–3, MSG.
10. Psalm 103:14.
11. 1 John 4:18.

CHAPTER 11

1. Luke 19:10.
2. Matthew 4:19.
3. 2 Corinthians 5:18–20, NLT.

4. John 3:3.
5. John 3:16.
6. See John 5:1–9.
7. See Mark 5:1–20.
8. See Luke 9:1–2.
9. Matthew 28:18–19, NIV.
10. John 20:21, NIV.
11. See 2 Kings 2.
12. Michael Hunt, "Elijah and Elisha: Great Prophets of God," Agape Bible Study, 2013, https://www.agapebiblestudy.com/charts/Miracles%20of%20Elijah%20and%20Elisha.htm.
13. John 14:12, NIV.
14. Acts 1:4, NLT.
15. John 15:4, NLT.
16. 1 Corinthians 9:24, NLT.

CONCLUSION

1. John 17:3, NLT.
2. See Philippians 3:8.
3. John 16:13, NLT.

CONNECT WITH
PASTOR JONATHAN STOCKSTILL

jonathanstockstill.com

bethany.com

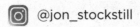 https://www.facebook.com/jonathan.stockstill

@jon_stockstill